T0301693

Small Stocks for Big Profits

*Generate Spectacular
Returns by Investing in
Up-and-Coming Companies*

GEORGE ANGELL

WILEY

John Wiley & Sons, Inc.

Published by John Wiley & Sons, Inc., Hoboken, New Jersey.
Published simultaneously in Canada.

For general information on our other products and services or for technical support, please contact our Customer Care Department within the United States at (800) 762-2974, outside the United States at (317) 572-3993 or fax (317) 572-4002.

Wiley also publishes its books in a variety of electronic formats. Some content that appears in print may not be available in electronic books. For more information about Wiley products, visit our web site at www.wiley.com.

Library of Congress Cataloging-in-Publication Data

Angell, George.
    Small stocks for big profits : generate spectacular returns by investing in up-and-coming companies / George Angell.
        p. cm.
    Includes index.
    ISBN 978-0-470-29665-3 (cloth)
    1. Small capitalization stocks.   2. Stocks.   3. Small business–Finance.   I. Title.
    HG4971.A54 2008
    332.63'22–dc22

                                                                        2008014651

Printed in the United States of America.

10   9   8   7   6   5   4   3   2   1

Contents

Preface

About 10 years ago, I had the luckiest day of my investment career. I received a phone call from a fellow in Las Vegas who made a living investing in small-cap stocks. We discussed the markets for a bit, trading background information. Did I ever come out to Las Vegas? the caller inquired. Sure. I enjoyed an annual trip to the gambling capital. I liked to bet on sports and the occasional craps game. Indeed, I had a trip to Las Vegas already planned for the following month. He suggested I look him up. We could have lunch. I made a mental note of our conversation and went back to whatever I was doing.

Five weeks later, I took a cab over to his Las Vegas office just before noon. We had lunch. And, as our discussion about the markets continued, we later had dinner. The entire day had been taken up with talk of his—and now my—foremost investment passion, the buying and selling of small stocks. This was an eye-opening event for me. In the years that followed, we invested in approximately a half-dozen stocks. Each of them proved to be a winner. And I mean a big winner. One, a small Vancouver-based mining company known as First Quantum Minerals (FM.TO), later soared from just 80 cents a share (where we bought it) to over $100 a share! The other stocks—mostly mining, gaming, biotech, and oil issues—returned more modest gains, but never failed to at least quadruple or quintuple in value. He was a firm believer in loading the boat. Constantly buying up 9 percent of the shares of these little-known companies (in order to stay under the 10-percent reporting limits for insiders), he usually owned a larger piece of the company than the key officers and board of directors combined. Needless to say, he earned millions. I made less, of course, because my investment commitment was on a more modest scale. But just recently, one of his little gems rose a whopping 42 percent in one day on discovery of gold on its Ontario property. It is getting so that I'm not even surprised by these spectacular winners anymore. But I know one thing: I could never find anyone to pay me this kind of money that I'm making in small stocks.

What is his secret? There isn't any secret. It is simply hard work. Being a confirmed dyed-in-the-wool value player, he seeks hidden value in everything he buys. Quite often, these hidden gems have value written all over them, but most hapless investors are too blind to the possibilities to risk taking a chance on an unproven, low-priced stock. You don't believe me? Turn on CNBC and monitor the stocks that they highlight all day long. You'd be hard-pressed to find one that triples or quadruples in value over six months. Yet these kinds of percentage gains are routine in the world of small stocks. Moreover, for a variety of reasons, the bonanza in small stocks is just beginning. In the coming three years, we should see unprecedented gains in the prices of small stocks as entrepreneurs seek out new opportunities in the fields of alternative energy sources, biotech advances, and technology. These modern-day explorers will be requiring financing by issuing shares in new companies that will undoubtedly see their fortunes—and share prices—grow. We are only at the bottom floor, the very beginning, of this exciting time in the investment world.

For the would-be investor in these up-and-coming stocks, the challenge remains daunting. How do you pick a winner? The fact is: Many of these opportunities exist in start-ups, unproven companies that have never earned a dime before. Anyone can ask their broker to recommend a dividend-paying blue-chip stock. But how do you put a price on someone's dream? Needless to say, there are people out there building a better mousetrap. I can remember back in the 1960s when a college professor told our class that "hi-fi" couldn't get any more advanced. Recently, I purchased an iPod the size of a pack of matches that holds virtually my entire CD collection—a collection, incidentally, that occupies a sizable portion of the shelving space in my media room. Who says the better mousetrap builders aren't out there today, utilizing new technologies that were unheard of even several years ago? The challenge, therefore, becomes one of finding these hidden opportunities and putting our money on the line. The payoffs will be impressive.

WHY ANOTHER STOCK MARKET BOOK?

I've been reading books on trading stocks, futures, and options for more than 40 years. Indeed, I've even written close to a dozen books on Wall Street. But not one of them prepared me for what I learned in the first two weeks as a pit trader on the floor of one of the Chicago exchanges. The theory is one thing; the reality of risking your money is quite another.

Not long ago, when I glanced through the pages of a number of investment books at my local bookstore, I noticed how useless most of the well-meaning advice was for the beginning investor. The books told the reader to diversify, as if that were the answer to finding the best stock. This, in fact, is known as the "spaghetti" technique, in which you throw a bunch of wet spaghetti against a wall to see what sticks. Similar investment books sang the praises of mutual funds or dollar cost averaging, in which you willy-nilly keep buying regardless of the wisdom of your stock selection. This latter piece of advice is given in hopes that the market will subsequently rise. What about not purchasing a bad stock in the first instance? There are a variety of ways in which stocks tell their stories. One is when a formerly quiet company suddenly experiences overwhelming share volume. There are other technical clues. But a stock's story may be highlighted in something as simple as excessive insider buying by company officers and directors. These individuals, who are closest to the company, are often the ones who buy and sell significant blocks of shares just before a market-moving event. There are ways to read the footprints of the insiders for those in the know. One such good indication is worth a dozen guesses. When you think about it, you need only a few good stocks to make a significant amount of money.

In the pages that follow, I've tried to outline some of the best ways to find undervalued, low-cost stocks. If you are a believer in the conventional wisdom, chances are you will have to turn everything you've learned until now on its head. As in any business, the cream rises to the top; only the few win the lion's share of the profits. The rest scramble for what's left over. The reason for this rests with human psychology. It is not that most people want to lose money in the stock market—only that most people are so risk-averse that they almost guarantee a negative outcome. Given a ground-floor opportunity, most people would rather wait until their profit is a certainty—a virtual prescription for trading losses. Once everyone knows a stock is worth buying and has done so, it is inevitable that the stock will decline. Witness the enthusiasm for buying stocks at the top.

THE SPECULATIVE VERSUS THE SURE THING: THE CRAY RESEARCH STORY

Most of today's stock market successes were created by companies that started small. The reason you keep hearing about the Microsoft millionaires is because they purchased or were given stock when the company was in its infancy—and dirt cheap. But the opportunity to make the real money in a stock like Microsoft is now over. Such a stock, which has undoubtedly minted hundreds of millionaires, is strictly a ho-hum affair today. The bloom is off the rose. The big opportunity has passed. The rule is you have to get there early.

The value of finding one good speculative stock comes home to me when I think of this true story that was told to me by a former New York

University student who went into the brokerage business. After graduating from business school, my friend became a stockbroker in New York City. After working in New York for several years, he decided to take a position with a brokerage firm in La Jolla, California. New to the West Coast, he took what business came his way while building his book, which later consisted of strictly high-net-worth individuals willing to put up millions in investment funds. At any rate, a retired schoolteacher appeared in his office one day, looking to invest $10,000 in the stock market. The broker recommended an investment in an up-and-coming high-tech company known as Cray Research, a computer company. My broker friend explained that on the one hand Cray was a risky investment and the teacher could lose all his funds. On the other hand, the broker said, there was a considerable upside. At the time, little-known Cray traded on what was known as the over-the-counter market. This was a market for lesser-known stocks that didn't qualify for the Big Board. Years later, of course, the over-the-counter market morphed into what is known today as the Nasdaq.

After careful consideration, the schoolteacher agreed to buy the stock and wrote a check for $10,000. The stock was purchased and placed in the teacher's account.

Several years passed.

Focusing on high-net-worth individuals, the broker lost contact with the schoolteacher and began seeking out promising stock opportunities for his wealthy clients. His business grew and he prospered. Finally, after a number of very successful years, the broker decided he wanted to start his own public company and get out of the brokerage business. But before he could leave his job, he had to call all his clients and tell them about his impending move.

That's when he called the schoolteacher.

"Oh, it's you!" the teacher responded when the broker called. "I'm not interested in buying any more stock."

The broker explained that he wasn't suggesting the teacher buy more stock. He just wanted to tell him that he was leaving the firm and another broker would have to handle his account.

"What are you talking about?" the teacher demanded. "The stock went to zero. It is not even listed in the newspaper anymore."

"Zero?" responded the broker. "What are you talking about? You own Cray Research."

"Well, it's not in the newspaper."

"Not in the newspaper?" said the broker. "Go get the newspaper and bring it to the phone."

The teacher did as he was told. The broker explained that the stock had split numerous times over the years and was now traded on the New York Stock Exchange—not over-the-counter. In fact, the teacher's shares were now worth well over a million dollars. The broker explained that he would be happy to sell the shares and place the funds in a mutual fund. The teacher couldn't believe his good fortune. For years thereafter, the broker received big baskets of fruit and candies every holiday season from his former client, who greatly appreciated his investment advice.

The broker later learned that the million-dollar bonanza changed the retired schoolteacher's life. It was a story he told with a great deal of pride.

HIDDEN GEMS

Finding similar opportunities is what this book is about. Not long ago, I went back and checked the performance of some of the stocks I recommended in my book, *The Best Small Stocks for 2007* (TradeWins Publishing). One mining issue, FNX Mining (FNX.TO) has gone from $10 a share to $30 a share. Zix Corporation (ZIXI), a stock that highlighted its potential by a number of volume spikes, has doubled in value this past year. Beas Systems (BEAS), a software maker, has risen smartly from under $14 to over $19 a share. Equinox Minerals (EQN.TO), a Toronto Exchange–traded mining issue, has risen from under a dollar to $4.70 a share. And, of course, Pelangio Mines Inc. (PLG.TO), which I purchased at about a dollar a share and was my stock of the year, is now trading above $4 a share. What these issues all have in common is that they were small, speculative stocks, with very little following in the investment community. They are now appearing on the radar screens of investors around the world. The key was identifying them before the crowd even noticed.

In the pages that follow, I spell out some of the key elements necessary to win in the market. Not only must you understand *what* stock to buy, but you must understand *how* to buy as well. Timing is everything in the market. Moreover, a premature purchase of a stock need not be a disaster. You can always average down, which is a time-honored tradition among stock market professionals.

I place a lot of emphasis in the book on entry techniques. The general rule is: The market will tell you when a stock wants to run. You simply must know what to look for. Moreover, once a stock tips its hand, it also offers you an opportunity to get aboard at a low-risk price—*if* you know what to look for. Take a quick look at Northgate Minerals Corporation (NXG). This was a stock that was a screaming buy at $2 a share (with virtually no downside risk). It is now trading at $3.35.

A lot of the book deals with time-tested support and resistance calculations. These are the same techniques that professional floor traders use—and you should as well. A stock forms a support pattern for a reason.

Investors think the stock is a good value at that price. That's why it makes so much sense to always know the support and resistance levels.

The issue of money management is addressed in a straightforward fashion. Anyone can be reckless and make money on a few lucky trades. But the professionals prefer to risk as little of their initial capital as possible, taking capital off the table and letting their paper profits ride. You'd be surprised how confident it makes one feel to know that regardless of the subsequent movement of the stock, you won't be taking a loss—because you got your seed capital out on the first move up. In a nutshell, professional traders become very proficient at doing one simple strategy. Then they repeat that investment strategy over and over again. The low risk is the key to their success.

Every successful trader will tell you that he or she has made a lot of mistakes over the years. In this department, I am no exception. But I find learning from mistakes is one of the best teachers around. Success tends to breed overconfidence. But failure requires that you examine your shortcomings and do something about them—if you intend to survive. There are a number of red flags that serve as a warning that something is wrong. I discuss some of them in the book. Unfortunately, however, the real lessons very often have to be learned firsthand, as you will see if you trade stocks for any period of time.

Whenever possible, I've tried to illustrate the principle with an example of an actual stock. In many of the examples, if I've traded the stock, I'll try to add my personal observations about what happened—for better or worse. I'm a big believer on stepping in when most other investors are heading for the exits. That's because I've had years of experience watching people panic at precisely the wrong time. There is a certain mob psychology that exists in the markets. Learn to understand it and you can be the one person standing amid a scene of wholesale destruction. It is especially gratifying to buy a stock near the bottom of its move only to see the price later skyrocket. Timing, indeed, is everything. It is so important that I've devoted an entire chapter to timing alone.

The challenge for the investor is to understand a stock's story long before the investment community becomes aware of its existence. In the beginning, you won't always know what you have. But if you work at it, you will find that a company's real value rests with its potential and not what the analysts and pundits are talking about. That's how I bought First Quantum Minerals (FM.TO) for about a buck a share before it headed to over $100 a share. It was also how I spotted Gigamedia (GIGM) before it skyrocketed. Remember, every stock has its story. It is just a question of figuring out which one is going to prove a bonanza down the road.

For the novice trader, I've included a crash course in technical analysis. Knowing the basics of technical analysis is vital to becoming a winning investor. Understanding chart patterns and time and price calculations is also important if you want to understand when to buy a stock and—significantly—when to sell. I devote a section to the most reliable patterns to look for. But the thing to remember is: A professional rarely guesses about a stock because he or she knows where the stock is heading based on the price patterns, which are clearly knowable to the discerning investor.

The longest chapter is devoted to exploring those strategies that are most likely to help you win. There are a number of pitfalls that you have to look out for. As you undoubtedly know, differences of opinion make the market. But it is downright uncanny how inaccurate most Internet-based opinion makers can be. My experience in buying Best Buy illustrates this phenomenon completely—right down to the point that these experts were saying Warren Buffett didn't know what he was doing. People love to buy a sure thing, of course. That's why I'm often out of a stock long before its name ever appears on CNBC.

Stock selection is mostly about separating the weak stocks from the strong ones. For this reason, I cover how to develop trading filters and how to use them. You'd be surprised how fine-tuning your strategies can put you in the winner's column almost immediately when you invest in a stock.

I devote a short chapter to the basics of capitalizing on initial public offerings. This is a specialty that may appeal to some investors, but, for most, it is better left alone.

One of my favorite topics is that of insider buying. When you have the combination of a rapidly falling stock price coupled with a massive buying program by someone within the company, it is almost always a sign that the next move is up. Shaking people out of the market is another time-honored tradition of the stock market. The problem is that if the "smart money" is buying, it is the worst possible time to sell. You'd be surprised how often the so-called fundamentals change overnight when negative news drags down a stock's price. The insiders know what is going on within a company. For them, buying or selling the stock isn't a speculative venture; they understand what is coming—sort of like when George W. Bush sold his shares in his small oil company right before the massive losses were announced. Fortunately, there is a way to track the footprints of the insiders.

Finally, there is a brief discussion of stock options and how to use option volume to pinpoint when to buy or sell a stock. You can also use options to obtain heightened leverage in a particular stock.

The "Road Map" chapter tries to tie everything together. Notice the price capitulation in Pelangio Mines Inc. at 30 cents. I own that stock, and today it is trading above $4 a share! Sometimes the best reason to trade small stocks is because it is simply so much fun! Here's to profitable trading.

NOTE

While every effort has been made to report the names and prices of the companies listed in this book accurately, it is important that the reader understands that nothing written here is an endorsement or recommendation to purchase a particular security. The key to investment success is timing. With a manuscript written so many months before the finished book gets into the reader's hands, it is impossible to present the current status of a particular stock as a buying or selling opportunity. Therefore, take the examples as they were meant to be used—as illustrations of specific strategies and nothing more. With a little work, the reader should be able to uncover his or her own examples.

Lastly, the material presented here is intended as a jumping-off place for the investor interested in buying and selling small stocks. It is not the final word. Neither the author nor the publisher should be held liable for investments made by readers of this publication since no legal, accounting, or other professional services are intended in this work.

CHAPTER 1

Making Money in Small-Caps

B y almost any benchmark, small-cap stocks are the new value on Wall Street—and, increasingly, on its counterpart in Canada, Toronto's Bay Street, where some of the highest fliers of the low-priced stock world trade. What's more, in the years to come, you'll find these hidden gems, these proverbial diamonds in the rough, leading the indexes higher. I say this with barely concealed enthusiasm because, given the current beaten-down investment climate, it is inevitable that the cycle will change and the small-caps will explode higher.

Small-caps present a ground-floor opportunity—one that doesn't present itself every day. We all know that expectations are the highest at market tops. But right now, because market expectations are less than stellar, the conditions are ripe for the astute investor to gobble up low-price shares in dozens of beaten-down companies whose stocks are selling significantly below their true value. Cheap stocks, depressed stocks, penny stocks, small-cap stocks—whatever you want to call them, they are the next new big thing. The question is: Will you get on at the ground floor, or would you prefer to wait until these shares sell at penthouse prices?

SMALL-CAPS: THE NEXT BULL MARKET

It's a simple premise: With the indexes already climbing to new highs, it is not a matter of *if* the next bull market will see a surge in small-cap stock prices, but *when*. Looking back, one can see plenty of historical evidence for continued explosive growth among low-priced stocks. Small-caps, for instance, have traditionally enjoyed spectacular gains compared with their higher-priced cousins. Over one recent 10-year period, small-caps outperformed larger-cap stocks by a whopping ten-to-one margin. As for percentage gainers, the small-caps invariably lead the pack. The top ten low-priced gainers increased in value by more than 261 percent over a recent year. During an identical period, the top ten S&P listed stocks gained just under 15.5 percent.

When you consider the numbers involved, you can see why investors prefer low-priced stocks. From an investor's standpoint, you can take $5,000 and buy 5,000 shares of a $1 stock (commissions excluded) or 100 shares of a $50 stock. A 50-cent gain in the $1 stock would generate $2,500 in profit. That's a 50 percent gain. The same 50-cent gain on the $50 stock, however, would generate just $50 in profit. To double in value, a $1 stock has to rise to only $2. To generate the same percentage gain, a $50 stock has to trade at $100 a share. Now ask yourself which is more likely to happen: a $1 stock going to $2 or a $50 stock going to $100?

The reluctance of investors to jump on the bandwagon of a higher-priced stock explains why successful companies often have two-for-one splits. By offering twice as many shares to their investors, companies can enjoy greater investor participation by halving the share cost from, say, $60 a share to $30 via a stock split.

Investor enthusiasm for small-caps is likely to grow for many reasons beyond the price alone. Smaller companies are more likely to be start-ups or in the early stage of their development. This allows greater upside potential. A seasoned company, on the other hand, has far greater difficulty in achieving the same level of growth as a new, smaller company. Accordingly, low-priced stocks can often double and triple in value while their big brothers have trouble attaining even a double-digit gain. It is not uncommon to see the stock of smaller companies increase in value by many hundreds of percent.

During uncertain times, however, these lower-priced companies are often ignored. People prefer something tried-and-true, perhaps a blue chip that pays steady dividends. The result is a lot of hidden value in the lower-priced issues. These are the shares we want to go prospecting for, sort of like digging up gold that lies hidden in the mine. Not surprisingly, many small-caps are indeed mining companies, their resources literally lying in the ground.

I found just such a stock several years ago when a friend recommended a little-known company trading on the Toronto Stock Exchange. Though its corporate offices were headquartered in Vancouver, British Columbia, First Quantum Minerals (FM.TO) was really an undiscovered asset-rich little copper-mining company in Zambia (see Figure 1.1). Its hidden value lay in its vast reserves still underground. The shares were then changing hands for just 80 cents Canadian. Within three years, a bull market in copper pushed the stock to more than $48 a share!

Although this stock has already made its run, you can be certain that many similar opportunities are out there. Moreover, the opportunities are not limited to just one sector or another. You might seek your fortune in mining or biotech or technology or dozens of other industries. There truly are opportunities everywhere!

SEPARATING THE WHEAT FROM THE CHAFF

In the pages that follow, I spell out a number of concepts and theories on how best to identify value in small stocks. I cover in detail the two most popular approaches to traditional stock market interpretation: fundamental and technical analysis. My approach is to find bargains based on price,

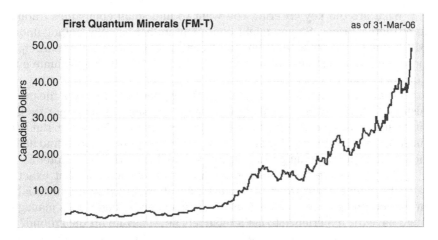
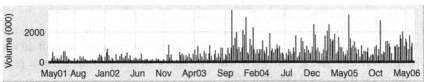

FIGURE 1.1 First Quantum Minerals
Courtesy of the Toronto Stock Exchange.

value, and market activity. Whether you call it buying low, buying cheap, or simply buying depressed stocks, you want to find the overlooked company that promises an impressive return. We are not looking to flip stocks. Your time horizon could be several weeks, months, or even years. It all depends on how you can best capitalize on a legitimate growth spurt. For investors who know where to look, the highest profits come from small companies with big prospects, so that is the area where we will concentrate our efforts. I hope you will find the guidelines easy to understand and implement.

You will learn how to evaluate and interpret performance: the best time to purchase—or sell—a given stock. You will also learn why some stocks fail to live up to their promise. You will discover the hidden pitfalls of investing—the most common mistakes made by just about every investor.

Over the years, I have looked at literally thousands of stocks. There are many stocks that, while they may look promising at first glance, upon analysis, don't measure up to our chosen criteria. We look at them from both a fundamental and a technical viewpoint. From a sample of more than 1,000 stocks, for example, you might select just 50 for additional analysis. This number then might be cut in half, and you'll ultimately end up with 15 to 20 high-probability selections. This task can be daunting, but it is necessary if you are to capitalize on the best opportunities.

What are the key criteria? You want to find small companies trading at attractive prices. So you might limit your study to stocks trading under $10 a share. You want the company to enjoy some measure of participation from the investment community. So you will take trading volume into consideration.

I try to avoid initial public offerings (IPOs) because they lack the price history that is crucial in making intelligent decisions. This is not to say there aren't wonderful opportunities in the IPO market. There are. But you must know what to look for and when to take the plunge. You'll find additional information about getting started in the IPO market in Chapter 5.

Then there are the all-important fundamental factors. What exactly does the company do? Does its business plan allow it to grow exponentially in the months and years ahead? Is its management sound? Does management have the experience to get a relatively new start-up off the ground? If the company has been in existence for a period of time, are there reasons for it to take off in the future? And so on.

On a technical level, a whole host of technical indicators measure whether a stock is performing correctly. I don't necessarily rule out an underperforming stock. But we'll want to know why the stock cannot pass muster on these vital benchmarks.

Learning what to look for takes time. Once you understand the key guidelines to stock selection, however, you'll be able to make both sound and quick decisions concerning a stock's viability.

HIDDEN VALUE: THE SMALL STOCK'S
SECRET WEAPON

If you want to make a small fortune, goes the old saying, start with a large fortune. In the world of small stocks, however, the key to making a small fortune is hidden value. What does the company have that could make its shares explode in value? In the case of First Quantum Minerals, the key was its vast copper reserves in a country set in the middle of political strife. Although the Zambian authorities have become increasingly pro-business in recent years, the same could not be said for some of its neighbors, notably the Democratic Republic of the Congo (DRC). Just the possibility of a political coup from a hostile neighbor can understandably scare off investors. No one wants to invest in a company that might one day be nationalized.

At times, the clues to a stock's potential can be subtle. While researching First Quantum, I learned that despite the possibility of neighboring government intrusions, the company had a good record in dealing with its employees. It operated a small hospital, for example, to provide its workers with health care. Didn't it make sense to conclude that a company that cared for its workers might also look out for the interests of shareholders? No fly-by-night operation would go to the trouble to construct a hospital. This company planned to be around for a while—truly, a positive sign.

At about the same time, an interesting article appeared in the *New York Times* that cited a surge in the growth of private golf courses in Southern Africa. What exactly is the connection between golf courses and mining? It seems that during the political turmoil of earlier times, private golf courses had been shut down as their members fled Africa. More often than not, these private clubs' membership included the managerial class of Africa's leading firms. These management professionals were precisely the people needed to generate business revenue, yet they had been driven out of the region because of political unrest. Now they were returning. According to the *Times* article, the new pro-business climate was generating renewed interest in leisure activities in the region, golf being just one of them. With the European managerial class returning, a new day had broken.

This change was subtle perhaps, but it didn't take me long to draw the logical inference. One, here's a company with vast undeveloped resources. Two, the company actually seems to take an interest in the welfare of its employees. Three, the influx of quality management professionals was on the upswing, as evidenced by the boom in local golf courses.

The fourth major point was as yet unknown. What was the potential for metal prices—specifically, the price of copper? If this company had what it promised, everything was in place for a phenomenal investment. The worldwide demand for the red metal soared. Share prices for the Zambian copper company went from under a buck to over $26!

If you are looking for a similar bonanza, you have to sense the potential before it becomes evident. One place to look is at biotech start-up firms. Though obviously fraught with risk (almost all of these firms have no profits in the beginning), these companies often double or triple in price when a breakthrough drug or diagnostic cure is introduced or, better yet, approved by the regulatory authorities. Take the case of one such stock I owned last year. The biotech firm Biomira (BIOM) surged from 80 cents to close to $3 a share almost overnight following a favorable ruling on one of its drug studies (see Figure 1.2).

Another biotech Canadian firm, DiagnoCure (CUR.TO), specializing in the development of proprietary diagnostic tools, likewise had a meteoric rise, soaring from $1 to over $6 a share, when it introduced its proprietary prostate test kit (as shown in Figure 1.3). At the same time, the Quebec City–based Canadian firm partnered a deal with San Diego–based Gen-Probe, which specializes in distribution of medical diagnostic equipment. Just recently, Gen-Probe has become a darling of Wall Street, making new highs day after day. Can it be long before little DiagnoCure is likewise discovered?

These companies are examples of what an intelligent investor looks for in terms of value. Timing is critical if you are to participate in the lion's share of the profits available in these and other stocks. But they illustrate

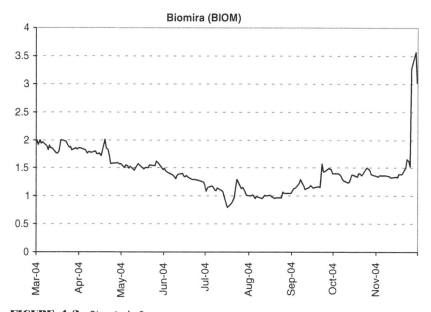

FIGURE 1.2 Biomira's Surge

FIGURE 1.3 DiagnoCure's Rise
Courtesy of the Toronto Stock Exchange.

the potential—*if* you are selective when you buy and sell. At the same time, remember that despite good intentions, even the best companies often encounter roadblocks and obstacles. Rare is the investor who hasn't been knocked around and blindsided by an unexpected earnings report. Even the best companies underperform occasionally. So the road to profitability is not always a carefree course. If you concentrate on finding hidden value, however, you will find that what a company has often prevails in the end.

THE VALUE INVESTOR

Not long ago, I spoke with a friend of mine who is a private investor. His strategy: buy little-known companies with good fundamentals. A self-described value investor, he understandably wants to buy before a company's story gets out.

"It always makes me a little nervous," he explained, "if there is a lot of interest when I buy."

His strategy is to buy shares in small, yet-to-be-discovered companies that have verifiable resources (mines and oil companies), emerging technologies (biotechs), or simply a rock-solid balance sheet in a hot sector (gaming). He may contact the CEO of a potential investment company and invite him over for lunch. When the CEO of a small company sees that someone is about to invest several million dollars in the company's stock, you'd be surprised how receptive he can be to such an invitation. One such investor brings not just his personal capital to the table but also the capital of his well-financed friends. He supports the stock in the truest sense of the word.

Over lunch, the conversation invariably turns to the company's hidden value.

"Mr. CEO," the investor might say, "I've been looking for an opportunity and was wondering if you were interested in greater investor support."

"Who wouldn't be? The company is hardly on the radar screens of most brokers right now."

"I understand, Mr. CEO. But without disclosing any inside information, what can you tell me about your mining operations at Silver Lake Ridge? What are the prospects, in your opinion?"

In this fashion, the sophisticated investor can gain a greater handle on the company, see firsthand whether the company's story seems to make sense, and see if the two of them make a good fit. An enlightened management will make an effort to accommodate such a request from a credible source.

Why?

There are many reasons. As the holder of perhaps hundreds of thousands of cheap shares, the CEO wants to get the company's story out there in front of the investment community. He may have a new IPO planned. He understands that his interests and the shareholders' interests are the same.

From the investor's standpoint, there may be questions he needs answered before he commits his capital. At this stage, the discussion might be just a fishing expedition. The investor might just want to get to know management first. Can he trust these guys? Do they seem upfront and honest? Do they have what they say they have? Are they just blowing smoke? What, in short, is the hidden value?

TIMING

Even the best stocks make lousy investments if you buy them at the wrong time. To decide when to buy—and sell—you must rely on technical price patterns. More art than science, technical analysis enables the astute investor to uncover a sleeping giant long before it springs awake. Several months ago, I performed a cursory analysis on several dozen stocks. Knowing my criteria, I quickly sped through the stock charts. Suddenly, I found what I'd been looking for: the classic bowl or saucer pattern. According to Figure 1.4, this little-known petroleum company was screaming, "Buy! Buy! Buy!"

By almost any measurement, little Abraxas Petroleum (ABP), trading on the American Stock Exchange, was poised to run. The chart pattern was a classic buy. The stock had done all the necessary sideways work. The next move was up. I bought it immediately.

Trading under $1.50 a share, the stock doubled in value in three months' time. But that was just the beginning. It later traded up to $9.25 a share!

You have probably never heard of little Abraxas Petroleum and many of the other stocks that might be discussed in this book. But ask yourself this: When was the last time that Disney, IBM, Motorola, or Lucent—not to mention dozens of other high-profile shares—doubled in value in three months? Granted, these stocks were all darlings of Wall Street at one time. Lucent, which often leads the most active list, once traded over $80 a share. More recently, it has traded as low as $2. Rather than concentrating on the past glories of these well-known companies, why not seek out

FIGURE 1.4 Abraxas Petroleum: Ready to Buy?

the new—and yet undiscovered—low-priced shares that might be in the headlines in the months and years ahead?

Small stocks routinely make percentage gains unheard of among larger stocks. In the past 12 months, the large-cap Dow stocks gained just 5 percent while the Russell 2000 index, which tracks the performance of small-cap stocks, registered a healthy 24 percent gain. Moreover, to the knowledgeable investor, they signal not just when and where to buy but exactly where to take profits as well. It's all a question of timing.

Investors are a remarkably impatient lot. When they purchase a stock, they often think that the stock should understand that their investment should trigger rapid price gains. In the case of low-priced stocks, which are often in turnaround situations (often that's why the price is low), a company's shares may drift lower for months and even years before the company's fundamentals change sufficiently for a sustained rally to begin. A distressed stock may take as long as one or two years forming a bottoming pattern on the charts. The good news is that this bottom pattern provides a strong foundation for the subsequent rally. But the investor must be patient.

A stock does not rise in value in isolation. Even the best companies are often beaten down by a bad market. Factors like high interest rates, deteriorating corporate profits, and a government with a reckless fiscal policy can all wreak havoc on the stock market. The thing to remember is that the market is cyclical. So today's dog is tomorrow's high flier. Anyone familiar with the doom-and-gloom mentality of a bear market can readily see how the fundamentals often seem to change overnight. A quick glance at the headlines of the *Wall Street Journal* often reveals this pattern. Last week's "Stocks Plunge on Interest Rate Rise" often becomes this week's "Stocks Soar on Improving Corporate Profits" headline.

The time element is crucial to sensible investing. Profitable investing requires having the vision to allow time for your investment to work out. With time on your side, you can readily grab shares at bargain basement prices—shares that are being sold by impatient and uninformed individuals who see the market as an alternative to this week's lottery.

SMALL STOCKS, BIG PROFITS

A low stock price enables you to purchase a lot of shares, often at a discount from the stock's true value. Several years ago, a friend called and said he had purchased a million shares of a little-known mining company then trading at $1 Canadian on the Toronto Stock Exchange. Virginia Mines (VIA.TO) was the classic asset play. It was a resource company poised to run higher on a boom in commodity prices. The stock is currently trading over $15 a share—not bad for a company that I was able to pick up for close to a buck Canadian, about 76 cents U.S. at the time. See Figure 1.5.

Not long ago, we stood outside his waterfront home on the West Coast of Canada, surveying his lawn that swept down to the sea. It was a truly magnificent setting, something right out of *The Great Gatsby*.

As we were enjoying the view, my friend turned to me and asked, "Do you remember Virginia Mines?"

"Yes. You were the one who first recommended it to me."

"Little Virginia paid for most of this house."

Here was a small stock that had provided a big payoff. When you buy with hidden value in mind, your profit is assured—if not today, certainly tomorrow or in the near future. The profit exists at the time you buy. That's why the hidden value approach is so profitable. Using this formula, you can string together a series of impressive wins. Not long ago, I reviewed a series of buys and sells that this same friend had recommended over a period of eight years. There were six prime selections that met all the technical and fundamental criteria. They were all winners. And of course, they all started out as small, underpriced stocks.

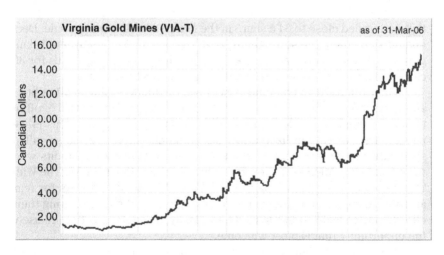

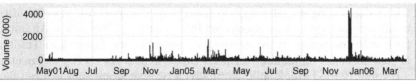

FIGURE 1.5 Virginia Mines: Classic Asset Play
Courtesy of the Toronto Stock Exchange.

I recently read an insider stock report that claimed you can't make money buying stocks under $5 a share. In fact, according to this insider, most stocks under $5 never rise above that price. Among the many misconceptions about the stock market, this attitude of avoiding low-priced stocks at all costs is just one of them. Another is the notion that price/earnings ratios are particularly helpful in selecting a stock. Indeed, some of the best low-priced stocks don't have any earnings at all—yet!

Two stocks that readily come to mind are Taser International (TASR) and Sirius Satellite Radio (SIRI) (see Figure 1.6). Neither stock had earnings when they were low-priced stocks, yet they both skyrocketed in price! Wouldn't you prefer getting in on the ground floor before anyone else has even heard of the stock?

Look how Taser stock traded from 50 cents to $9.

PAYING PENNIES, SELLING FOR DOLLARS

Selecting low-price stock opportunities requires looking for unique situations or promising fundamentals. Several years ago, I found a mining stock that had traded close to $4 a share in the March 2000 Internet bubble. Decimated since then, the stock tumbled all the way to 6 cents, where it languished. By the time I discovered this stock, it was changing hands for 30 cents a share—a fivefold increase. It later rose to $2.18 a share.

When you have an emerging asset play, the hidden value is often literally underground. In a situation like this, the company's potential is often underestimated or overlooked by the investment community. This is especially true when you have a low-priced stock because these so-called speculative issues are beneath the dignity of the Wall Street pundits who want you to buy Microsoft, Motorola, and other sure-thing stocks. The Wall Street crowd won't even look at one of these speculative stocks for fear an enterprising attorney down the road will accuse them of steering their clients toward reckless investments. Ironically, these stocks offer precisely the opportunity that is most welcome.

Pardon the pun, but finding a mining company such as this one requires a little digging. Again, a friend who specializes in uncovering opportunities in little-known gems first uncovered the potential of this stock. An initial look at the company wasn't particularly positive (see Figure 1.7). Trading at just 15 cents Canadian, Northern Orion Resources (NTO) engineered a reverse 10-for-1 stock split. Normally, a reverse stock split is a red flag to an investor because it suggests that a company is about to be delisted on account of a low share price. The reverse split immediately raises the

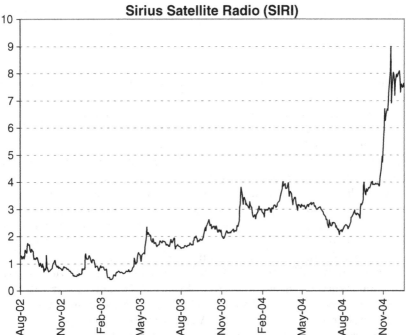

FIGURE 1.6 Taser International and Sirius Radio

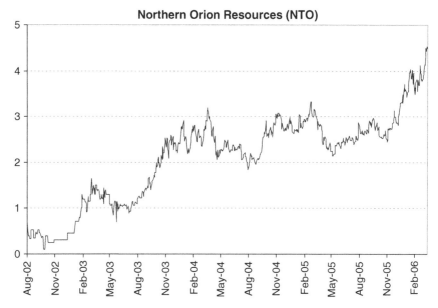

FIGURE 1.7 Northern Orion Resources

price, but typically the shares fall in value after this face-saving maneuver. In this instance, the reverse split meant the 15-cent shares were now valued at $1.50—but, remember, there are only a tenth as many shares. Instead of owning 1,000 shares at 15 cents apiece, the shareholder now had only 100 shares valued at $1.50 each. (Note that Northern Orion shares were subsequently listed at the American Stock Exchange; Northern Orion was later bought out by Yamana Gold.)

This little-known copper and gold producer, however, was not your typical reverse-split candidate. A glance at the fundamentals revealed a company on a positive growth spurt. The company had recently acquired 12.5 percent of the Alumbrera Mine in northwest Argentina. Partly because of the collapse of the Argentinean peso, this was one of the lowest-cost mines in the world to operate. At the same time, the worldwide demand for copper surged. The company's 2004 share in Alumbrera was 49 million pounds of copper and 71,000 ounces of gold. Even greater amounts of these metals have been discovered in the Alumbrera Mine since then.

So profitable did their operations become, largely based on the Alumbrera Mine windfall, that Northern Orion had a corporate nest egg of more than $140 million. Eighteen months after the reverse split, the shares traded over $4, creating an impressive reward for the shareholders as well as the company. I want to stress that I have long since taken profits in this little gem. But there are other promising situations on the radar screen.

EVERY STOCK HAS ITS STORY

As you can probably tell by now, every stock has its story. I've tried to highlight just a few here. The key, of course, is finding out the story before it becomes widely known. You'd be surprised how prosaic some of the biggest success stories are. Who would have thought that a chain of hardware stores would morph into Home Depot? Or that the notion of discounting would create a Wal-Mart empire? Or inexpensive hamburgers, the McDonald's chain? I am not saying, of course, that the investment world isn't full of pitfalls for the unsuspecting investor. Mark Twain once quipped that a mine was a hole in the ground with a liar standing on top. The same might be said of numerous dry oil-drilling ventures, as well as many other areas where investors have lost money in the past.

You truly don't always know what you have when you begin to investigate the prospects of a given investment. But separating the wheat from the chaff is what this story is all about. The payoff comes when you discover a treasure trove of unrealized opportunity. That's our goal here.

In the pages that follow, you will see that I rarely concentrate on traditional guidelines for picking successful stocks. There is a pattern for finding the kind of hidden gems we are talking about here, but you won't find the analysts on CNBC discussing these stocks. They are, frankly, too speculative for the television pundits, who are more interested in covering familiar companies like Disney, General Motors, IBM, and Coca-Cola. I am confident in saying that these high-priced, seasoned stocks will never register the percentage returns of low-price stocks. By the time a stock becomes a household name, you can bet its story has entered the folklore of the investment community. We are looking for the untold story, the story yet to be highlighted on the front pages of the *Wall Street Journal*.

This iconoclastic view is not shared by everyone. But for aggressive investors who don't want to spend their investment hours chasing small returns, this focused and specialized approach makes sense.

Finally, you must also understand that finding the best opportunities requires hard work—and a bit of luck. Let's get started.

CHAPTER 2

Getting Started in Technical Analysis

T here are just two approaches to stock market analysis: so-called fundamental analysis, which concentrates on supply-and-demand factors influencing a stock's price, and technical analysis, which looks at a stock's price history and trading patterns. To be fair, most analysts will tell you that they look at both fundamental and technical factors in analyzing a stock. But a smaller number will swear by just one, defending their stance as the only legitimate way to ascertain a stock's true value. I prefer the Chinese menu technique of taking some from group A and some from group B.

Regardless of which approach you ultimately select, it is helpful to have at least a cursory knowledge of both fundamental and technical analysis. I'm not trying to present a comprehensive discussion here. Rather, I'm laying the groundwork for the material we will cover later. If you haven't had exposure to stock market analysis, perhaps this material will whet your appetite for additional study. Many good books that cover these techniques in greater depth are available. In this chapter, we'll just cover the basics.

If the term *technical analysis* sounds imposing, don't be concerned. Although technicians—also known as *chartists*—have their own nomenclature, these mysterious names, like so much in the stock market, are typically just shorthand. A technician will talk about a stock having support or resistance after breaking out of an ascending triangle. If you feel lost in reading language like this, don't be. Once mastered, these terms are easy to understand. More important, they often pinpoint important areas where a stock may churn—move sideways—prior to a significant move.

Those with a mathematical bent will naturally be drawn to technical analysis, which on one level attempts to reduce price action to a mathematical number. With so much emotion typically associated with a given stock's performance, this is clearly impossible, but it doesn't prevent technical adherents from trying to quantify price action.

As with so much in the stock market, the technician's pursuit is often made to look overly complicated. Newer traders are most often fearful of easily mastered subjects when, in fact, the real challenge is simply putting down one's money in a speculative venture. Whereas the former can be learned, the latter is more apt to be charged with emotion. There is no doubt that you can learn to understand technical analysis. But it is far more difficult to convince you to buy 10,000 shares in a 50-cent stock that you fear may fall to zero. The same stock may also soar to $3 or $4 a share. But that is little consolation to new traders who cannot see the hidden value in their low-priced shares.

The real task comes with trying to tie together a series of different, yet related, indicators and coming up with some sort of coherent approach to the market. That's why technical analysis is part art, part science. Technicians will never escape fundamentalists' claim that they are just reading tea leaves. The technician's complaint, of course, is that all the stock's supply-and-demand parameters are factored into the price.

Technical analysis, in the sense that it measures price movements, is the best method to analytically understand the market. Ideally, when you perform a technical assessment of the market, you are dealing with the facts and not your sometimes volatile emotions. The facts can tell you, for instance, how far a rally might go before encountering serious resistance. Alternatively, the facts might tell you how far a countermove might carry following a significant rise. These facts can be marshaled and analyzed. Once understood, the facts must be acted upon by the technician who is attempting to make sense of the market.

At all times, the analyst must take into account the notion of risk in the market. Not to acknowledge risk is like not acknowledging the chance that cancer might be present in our bodies. That's why your doctor recommends an annual checkup. Moreover, it must also be acknowledged that risk is often commensurate with reward. If it is safety you seek, your rewards are unlikely to equal those of people who embrace riskier ventures. When it comes to low-priced stocks, the gains can exceed 100 percent in a short period. But every once in a while, the buyer of low-priced stocks picks a company that faces bankruptcy, and the entire investment is lost. As a rule, superior rewards are available only to those who take on substantial risk. So if this game is for you, make sure you are comfortable with the risk involved. You can make every effort to minimize your risk exposure in purchasing a stock, but that risk component cannot be entirely factored out. Indeed, perhaps the best strategy is simply embracing the risk as part and parcel of the investing experience.

THE CONVENTIONAL WISDOM

You might want to acknowledge risk by thinking of the market as a giant paradox. That's because so much of the conventional wisdom is turned on its head when it comes to taking a flier on a low-priced stock. Take the notion of low-priced stocks being outlandishly risky. Is it safer to invest in a company with an emerging technology? Sirius Satellite Radio (SIRI) is an example that comes to mind. Or would you prefer a tried-and-true blue chip that's been hyped to the moon by a clannish investment community? In a sense, you could say the idea comes from the Bible. The concept that the last shall be first, and the first shall be last is routinely proven in the high-stakes investment world of low-priced stocks. After all, these tend to be unpopular and forgotten investments that are hardly the buzz on Wall Street. But when you look to the bottom line, which, of course, is the sensible thing to do, this is where the money is made—in the little-known gems that later become household names.

Technical analysis is immune to popular trends. There have been technicians on Wall Street for more than 125 years. Yesterday's railroad stock may no longer be with us, but the price patterns created by yesterday's blue chips and today's biotechs are identical. Stocks still consolidate in support and resistance zones, and they still break out and soar in predictable patterns. Numbers are numbers, and that isn't going to change with the fashion of the day.

Technical analysis will provide you with numbers. The problem rests with deciding which ones to follow. This is not easy. If you are at all honest with yourself, you will agree that there are always two arguments to be made: one for higher prices and one for lower prices. In fact, if you can make only one argument, you are probably blinded by your love or distaste for a stock. Differences of opinion make the market. Nevertheless, you must charge ahead with a sensible trading plan.

The trading plan is the blueprint for where you want to go. Technical analysis provides the means for implementing the blueprint. In any sensible trading plan, you need guidelines to tell whether you are on track or off in moving toward your goal. Understanding the technical situation of a given stock will enable you to size up the chances for success or failure. Be aware that the successful investor must not only seek the best buying candidates but likewise avoid purchasing stocks that show signs of deterioration.

There is no denying that the technician faces a challenging task. How do you blend together such exotic indicators as stochastics and Fibonacci numbers with Bollinger bands and moving averages? Most analysts will tell you it is relatively easy because they all favor their own, often proprietary, indicators. While these indicators will almost certainly all have their day, the real question is this: Will they continue to work in the future?

Technical analysis has always played an important role in the selection of winning stocks. But only since the advent of personal computers has numbers-crunching become such an all-consuming process. Today in a few minutes you can perform an analysis on a stock that would have taken weeks 50 years ago. The result is a proliferation of financial trading systems. More important, it has taken much of the inefficiency out of the market. Opportunities that existed in the past are no longer available now because they are spotted and acted upon by alert traders who utilize computer power.

WHAT IS TECHNICAL ANALYSIS?

The fundamental factors tell us the facts about a company, and the technical factors tell us where the market's been, its relative strength or weakness. Simply put, technical analysis is the study of price movements. A technician wants to know whether a stock is being accumulated or distributed, whether the short interest is rising or falling, and whether the long-term trend is up or down, not to mention a dozen other measurements of a stock's health or lack thereof. Armed with sufficient knowledge, the technician attempts to stay one step in front of the crowd. Once the news is known, the opportunity has often passed, and "buy the rumor, sell the news" could be said to be the technician's mantra.

Ideally, the technical indicators can tell where the stock might be headed. They can also pinpoint a spot to enter and exit a market. The beauty of trading with technical indicators is that it really doesn't matter whether you trade commodities or stocks because the patterns are the same. They tend to be the same whether you trade low-priced or high-priced stocks or, for that matter, something that isn't a stock at all. Options, futures, stocks, even real estate prices—all can be charted and interpreted with technical analysis. Given sufficient volume and bullish chart patterns, you stand to make good money regardless of the underlying financial instrument. You just have to keep your wits about you and remember what we said about technical analysis being part science, part art. The challenge is when to put your faith in the art and when to put your faith in the science. Understandably, this can be daunting.

The fundamental factors influencing a stock are one thing, and the technical factors are another. Yet, a third factor—psychology—seems to have a hold on the market unlike any other. The unprecedented boom in stock prices in the late 1990s into the year 2000—and the subsequent break—showed the power that trader psychology holds over the market. In a perfect world, stocks would trade precisely at their intrinsic value based on the underlying fundamentals. Yet this is rarely the case. Instead, a stock often trades above or below its true value based on how investors perceive the company's chances for success or failure. In times of extreme optimism, a given stock's price gets ahead of its true value; the reverse is true when investors become pessimistic about the future. The silver lining in all of this is that astute investors can seize opportunities as investor psychology drives stock prices above or below their true value. Indeed, the entire rationale of purchasing low-priced stocks is to capitalize on an emerging situation that has not yet come to fruition.

The key to understanding technical analysis is to see how investors react to stock price changes. Do you really think that a stock market crash, such as the one during October 1987, really reflected the value of the underlying conditions? Why would a company lose billions of dollars in value in a single day? The fact is that the underlying companies didn't lose value, but clearly, the perception of a company's value may have indeed changed—if only for a short period. Just about all investors who held on following the 1987 crash saw their stock regain its value, and more. In the long run, therefore, the fundamentals are likely to prevail. But in the short run, we rely on technical analysis to provide a clue when a given stock is undervalued or overvalued.

WHERE TO BEGIN?

The most useful tool to the technician is the basic high, low, and close bar chart. You can study a weekly chart for the longer perspective, but this is just the starting point. A seasoned analyst will most certainly observe the hourly or 30-minute chart, and a day trader might consult a 5-minute chart. For most investors, the best place to start is the basic daily chart, where each day's trading activity is measured by a single bar.

Bar charts are typically constructed from a variety of indicators that are printed below or upon the same grid as the daily prices. These can get complicated, so it is best to begin with just price and volume. In the past, chartists constructed their own charts by hand using graph paper. Thankfully, those days are gone. With today's technology, you simply type in your stock symbol and whatever parameters you are interested in seeing.

The computer does the rest. Interested in how your stock traded today? Simply tell the computer to plot the chart. Let's see, it was up 5 cents in the morning, lost 2 cents by noon, and closed up 11 cents on the day. The chart will clearly show you what it did. You can just as easily plot a 5-day chart, a 1-month chart, a 3-month chart, or a 6-month chart. Given the lightning speed of computers, you won't lack for things to look at. The challenge, of course, comes with interpreting the chart patterns that are presented to you.

It won't be long before you begin to discover the relationship of stock prices and influencing factors. Take the relationship of stock prices to volume. Even a cursory study will reveal that stocks tend to rise or fall on high volume. A market that drifts lower on low volume is a lot different than a market that collapses on high volume. Indeed, you might say they would generate opposite signals. At a later point, we will discuss the specifics of trading with volume. For now, let's just say that trying to draw a conclusion about a stock's chances without looking at volume is akin to being a doctor who is trying to make a diagnosis without actually seeing the patient. It could be done, but not without significant risks.

The task for the technical analyst is to correctly grasp the clues that the charts are providing. Following a price rise on high volume, does the stock's selloff mean the move is over—or is it simply profit-taking? The daily chart often reveals the hidden footprints of the underlying forces in the market. Trying to discern the meaning of these patterns is the real challenge.

The basic chart, as we have mentioned, consists of high, low, and close price action plus volume. On a daily chart, a single bar represents one day's price action. But you can zoom in on a day by looking at 5- or even 1-minute bars, in which case, each bar represents a shorter time, depending on which time period you select. Conversely, you can zoom out and look at, let's say, weekly bars. The choice is yours. While there is much to be said for taking a comprehensive look at the market by observing a variety of charts, you want to be careful to not lose sight of the forest by looking at the trees. Remember the old story of a number of blindfolded people touching an elephant. Because each was in contact with only one part of the animal, each misinterpreted the elephant.

There are a variety of chart patterns that tend to repeat. Certain patterns can be very reliable and provide you with a clear-cut signal that prices are heading higher or lower. Other patterns are less clear and may suggest a sideways trend. With study, you will find that prices go through so-called consolidation phases, during which they are preparing to break higher or lower. Let's examine the most basic patterns that technicians routinely use to base their buy-and-sell decisions.

SUPPORT AND RESISTANCE

An examination of support and resistance is the logical place to begin any discussion of technical analysis. Support and resistance zones are much more common than dramatic moves higher or lower. Support points are the low prices that a stock reaches before turning around and heading up. A stock often rises enough to draw out sellers. The increased selling (whether profit-taking or short selling) often causes prices to decline to a level where buyers again enter the market. Their buying then supports the stock price, and prices cease to decline. This up-and-down pattern soon creates a support zone.

At the top of the zone, prices tend to cease rising when they encounter a resistance—a point where sellers put a stop to rising prices. At the resistance, the stock's buying power ceases to overwhelm the selling power, and prices tend to drift lower. In a nutshell, the support is where prices stop declining and the resistance is where prices stop rising.

To complicate matters, support and resistance points can change identities. A resistance zone, once penetrated, may become a new support zone. Conversely, a support zone, once penetrated, may become a new resistance zone.

The same principles that apply to a breakout or breakdown on a support level apply to a violation of a resistance. When a stock is ready to run, it violates the resistance and breaks out to a higher level. This breakout phenomenon also illustrates another important point about support and resistance. That is, contrary to the age-old adage to buy low and sell high, the market is never too high to buy and never too low to sell. By definition, a stock about to break through a resistance is trading above its recent trading range. To get aboard such a move, therefore, you may be required to buy at a price above recent price levels. If the market is indeed about to run, this should present no problem. Nevertheless, as you will see from the discussion that follows, this strategy is not without risks.

CHARTS AND TRENDLINES

There are three basic types of charts that most technicians use. The first is the *bar chart*, a single bar that represents the high, low, and close of a given time period. The bar can represent a given day's price, in which case it is known as a daily chart, or it can be shorter or longer in duration. You can have a 1-minute bar chart, with a separate bar for each minute of trading, or a 5-, 10-, or 30-minute bar chart, each representing a different time frame. On the other extreme, you can have weekly or monthly bar charts. A second kind of chart is known as a close-only *line chart*. This is a line representing the closing price over a period of time. A third type of chart is known as a *candlestick*. While the intricacies of candlesticks are beyond our scope here, be assured that many technicians swear by this ancient Chinese method of charting. A fourth chart type is known as a *point-and-figure chart*. This type of chart is also beyond the scope of this discussion. Regardless of which method of charting you use, you should be familiar with the most common patterns.

The notion of the trendline is the simplest concept to understand when you are tracking prices. Because prices tend to *trend* when they move higher or lower, technicians regularly draw in trendlines to illustrate the price trajectory. There are just a few things you need to know about trendlines. One, trendlines are drawn from lows in rising markets and from highs in declining markets. Two, when trendlines are broken, they tend to stay broken, meaning the trend has changed, from rising to falling, or vice versa. Three, the longer a trendline stays intact, the stronger it is likely to be. Finally, if the trendline is very steep, it is likely to be broken fairly quickly.

As a beginning chartist, you will want to observe many charts before you place your money at risk. What do these charts tell you? Can you identify a clear-cut trend? What about when the trend is broken? Does that spell the end of the move? With experience, you will begin to identify trends and see how prices adhere to a given upward or downward trajectory.

Chartists pay particular attention to trendlines. When prices approach an up trendline, buyers step in and purchase in anticipation of the line holding. The downside, of course, is that if the line is broken, there is inevitable selling on stops as investors attempt to exit the market as quickly as possible.

In summary, you want to remember the following:

The basics. Once a market begins to trend—either up or down—it forms a trendline. In an up market, the trendline is drawn from the lows going up. In a down market, the trendline is drawn from the highs going down. A penetration of a trendline is typically considered the end of the trend—if only temporarily.

Look for a violation of a trendline as a market signal. If you are looking to buy, a reliable pattern to look for is a downward trendline that has been violated. As prices deteriorate, more and more sellers enter the market, sending prices lower. After a time, the selling dissipates, and bargain hunters step in. Substantial accumulation of shares cannot occur without prices first stabilizing and then moving higher. Deteriorating markets are characterized by panic selloffs punctuated by sudden, explosive spikes. As a result, chartists must be careful when drawing in a down trendline. The trendline may be violated, followed by a quick resumption of the downward trend. The reverse, of course, is true when dealing with up trendlines.

The extremes are made quickly. A quick bottom reversal, following a prolonged downward trend, may be the key to higher prices ahead. At the bottom, a market is frequently deeply oversold; this suggests the selling has been overdone and the market is due for a sharp rebound.

BREAKOUTS

The *breakout* is a classical bullish pattern that occurs when the number and strength of the buyers overwhelms the sellers. As the name suggests, in breakouts prices move away from an area where they have been consolidating for a period of time. The corresponding bearish pattern is typically known as a *breakdown*. In the breakout, the accumulation of shares exceeds the distribution, and share values rise. The breakout is normally accomplished on a price gap when share values leave a space on the chart, which is often not filled. This unfilled gap on a chart is known as a *breakaway gap*.

The breakout is the simplest and most important pattern for the beginning chartist to know. By definition, a rising stock must take out its high. Buying the breakout, therefore, is one of the strongest possible buys a technical analyst can make. Unfortunately, the strategy is fraught with danger because, by definition, you are buying a new high amid a flurry of buying activity. The risk is that the breakout proves false and the market then subsequently trades back down into the so-called consolidation area between the resistance and support. A pattern that fails in this fashion is known as a *false breakout*. For the buyer of the breakout, this failure means trouble. The buyer may have just purchased near the top of the move. The failure of the move suggests the odds now favor prices trending lower. The best way to deal with this scenario is to immediately sell the position at a loss.

A more encouraging sign is a breakout accompanied by high volume. A high-volume breakout frequently means a legitimate move to the upside. Often news-driven, this breakout must be purchased immediately lest the investor be left behind. A typical scenario of a news-driven event culminating in a breakout is a better-than-expected earnings report released before the opening bell. With a mountain of buy orders bidding the stock higher, the opening price often gaps higher and runs. When this occurs, you have a breakaway gap. This breakout is the real thing. Timid investors who cautiously wait for something to push prices lower will be disappointed because their orders to buy will go unfilled.

Breakouts can be confusing to the novice trader who is unprepared for the fast and furious price action that often accompanies them. The breakout can be indicative of a *stop-running* operation in which the market is momentarily taken higher (in order to run the stops), only to be offered lower moments later when the initial buying flurry subsides.

As a new investor, you must understand this phenomenon. Stop-running means the market is purposely bid up in order to generate stop orders. When a market is bid into the stops, the stops, which are orders to buy at the market, generate buying activity. In this instance, the stop serves to protect the short seller (someone who borrows stock to sell in anticipation of buying back shares at a lower price). Should the market surge higher, short sellers find themselves in a lot of trouble because they must repurchase shares they sold short, regardless of price. Obviously, if they must pay a higher price than they sold at, they sustain a loss. Thus, short sellers place stop orders to protect themselves above the market. When the stops are run, market orders are thus triggered. This buying activity temporarily causes prices to rise as the stops generate buy orders from the short sellers. Once the buying dissipates, however, the market typically goes dead—and a freefall is likely.

As you may begin to realize, investors are on the horns of a dilemma when it comes to breakouts. On the one hand, if they fail to purchase immediately following a breakout, they may miss the subsequent move; on the other hand, if they are quick to join the buyers following a breakout, it may just be a stop-running exercise, and the market will collapse. So how do you decide? If you take the position, one of two things will occur: Either the position will be profitable immediately, or it will not. In the first instance, you have the right side; in the latter, you need to exit as quickly as possible.

If you hesitate following the breakout, however, you will typically miss the move. Breakout markets often follow weeks, if not months, of sideways price action, during which the bulls and bears are engaged in a prolonged struggle. When the market finally breaks and runs, that's the direction it is going to go. If you are hesitant following a breakout, one of three things will probably happen to you. One, you will chase the market. This suggests you will be paying more than you wished for the stock. Two, you will buy the high, meaning you will soon have paper (unrealized) losses. Three, you will miss the move entirely. As you can see, none of these alternatives is particularly attractive.

In summary, the investor must keep in mind the following four points:

1. **The breakout is often the beginning of a major move.** By definition, the breakout occurs at a higher price than that at which the market has been trading. Do not be afraid to pay up to get aboard a breakout. If it is a legitimate breakout, prices will continue to soar.

2. **Look for confirmation of the move.** While the breakout can be a powerful sign of a bullish scenario, the investor needs to be careful lest the breakout fails and prices fall into the consolidation area. The primary components of a breakout are price and volume. On a good breakout move, prices will be bid up, often on the open following a news event. The move will be accompanied by strong volume.

3. **Beware of false breakouts.** The move is not without its risks. A failed breakout results in immediate losses to the breakout buyers; if you are a buyer of a failed breakout, take the loss and exit the market immediately. The market *should* run on a breakout. If it doesn't, look elsewhere for an opportunity.

4. **The breakout is often a continuation pattern.** The breakout is often a confirmation of an established trend. The pattern typically occurs from a consolidation following the creation of a strong first leg. In this instance, the breakout signals the beginning of the second leg. Trends, as a rule, are comprised of two legs that are comparable in both time and price.

MANAGING THE BREAKOUT TRADE

Should you find yourself in the enviable situation of having purchased the breakout and see your stock rising, you mustn't grow complacent. As a rule, new traders are boldest when they should be cautious and most cautious when they should be bold. Quick, substantial profits are apt to be fleeting in the market. So you can bet that profit-taking, in the form of selling, will enter the market following any strong rally. At this point, you must make a decision concerning your position. There are many ways to determine where to take profits. A simple rule is to sell after three days up. Markets rarely have three higher closes without some selling driving the market lower, if only momentarily. If you take a long-term perspective, you may anticipate substantially higher prices. In that case, either hold on or buy more on the inevitable profit-taking break.

Aggressive traders understand that they must strike when the iron is hot. A 70-30 rule in the market says that 70 percent of the time the market is getting ready to move, or churning sideways. That leaves just 30 percent of the time when the market is moving from level to level, either up or down. In reality, it is probably more like 90-10, with the market moving up or down only 10 percent of the time. That's why you want to capitalize on a trending market. We are, of course, speaking in generalizations here. The market, as a whole, may be dead in its tracks. You want to care only if your particular stock is running.

It is hard for a new trader to be an aggressive trader. This takes time, especially because the new trader is apt to become aggressive at precisely the wrong time—at the very top when the equity is at the highest. The real place to become aggressive is when you've found the right buying opportunity in the right stock. Then, if there has been a setback in the market and profit-taking occurs, you have an added opportunity to buy more. Here you need to become flexible and buy weakness. As you may remember, on the initial gap up, you bought strength. This was the correct strategy. On the subsequent break, however, you now buy weakness. This is where you need to understand what is going on in the market.

Any run higher generates sellers. Weaker hands see this selling and think the move is over. Their selling is your buying opportunity. An aggressive buyer typically buys three times, depending on the movement of the stock price. First, you buy on the breakout. Second, you buy on profit-taking. Third, you buy any subsequent weakness. And that should be pretty much it. The third time should be the charm. If you buy three times and the market comes back on you, you may want to rethink your strategy—and perhaps bail out of the entire position. Once positioned, however, you now face yet another dilemma: Where should you sell? Before addressing that question, however, let's move on in our discussion of the most prominent chart patterns.

CONTINUATION AND REVERSAL PATTERNS

All chart patterns fall into just two classifications: continuation and reversal patterns. They mean, of course, precisely what they sound like, patterns that suggest a continuation of the trend once it completes itself and those that suggest the market is reversing direction. When you have support and resistance, the breakout usually suggests that the market will run in the direction of the breakout. But as we've already suggested, the reverse is also true when a false breakout occurs. Paradoxically, false breakouts can be particularly meaningful when your stock is about to make a strong rally or decline. For example, there might be a strong basing pattern, with the stock creating a strong support. Then you notice that the support is broken and the stock moves lower, often resulting in a selling frenzy. If prices move back up above the initial support, you have all the confirmation you need. The stock is headed significantly higher.

At a market top, the reverse occurs in a slightly different fashion. Stocks rarely base at the top. More likely, they soar higher on strong buying. When the buying gets overdone, short sellers (those who borrow stock to sell in anticipation of buying back lower) step in and aggressively sell, trying to push prices lower. Should the short sellers fail, they face an immediate and painful dilemma. They must buy to get out of their positions, lest their losses mount from the continued high prices. Once spooked, the short sellers panic. What you have then is a quick run up in which the shorts kill themselves to get out. This is known as a *short-covering* rally. More often than not, it is short-lived. The surest sign that the top has been reached is when the market simply goes dead. At that point, there is only one way the market will trade, which is down. So you can see that tops are made rapidly. That's why so few investors ever sell a stock at the very top.

Looked at another way, continuation patterns are simply way stations where the market ceases to rise prior to resuming the trend. But reversal patterns are dramatic. They are often made amid a frenzy of buying and selling when the outcome is far from certain for just about everyone involved. You have no doubt heard the old Wall Street adage that a bull market climbs a wall of worry. One trader described it as pushing a giant boulder up a hill. The downside, of course, is a different matter. Here the boulder falls off the cliff. That's when you get the October 1987 break or the March 2000 Internet bubble collapse. Traders should be understandably concerned when they hold stocks in long, sustained rallies. A single violation of a trendline can signal a massive selling frenzy.

Many analysts will tell you that violation of a trendline is the surest sign that a move is over. They'll be reluctant, however, to call a market one way or another prior to the breakout from a pattern. Without covering each in detail, you will hear these patterns referred to as pennants and flags, triangles, rectangles, diamonds, and saucers. All, without exception, are self-explanatory in terms of their shape. The number of times a stock stops at a key support or resistance is also important. So you will hear about double and triple bottoms and tops, as well as the so-called M and W formations. Again, all provide a handle for chartists to make sense of patterns that are often elusive and difficult to discern, especially in the early stages.

In any discussion of technical analysis, one thing is certain. Everyone is an expert after the pattern is formed. What seemed so elusive to just about everyone becomes a sure thing once the pattern reveals itself. Try to avoid falling into this trap—or, for that matter, listening to people who would have you believe they are experts based on past market behavior. Before the market broke that trendline, you, like everyone else, were patiently waiting for higher prices. The antidote to this type of thinking is to cultivate a series of measurements based on past market behavior that provides a certain future predictability of where prices should go. Anyone can *react* to a stock's behavior. It is far more useful, not to mention profitable, to be able to *predict* price behavior well in advance of the event. The real value of technical analysis is to use the tools to predict where the market will indeed trade.

As you may have discerned by now, technical analysis can provide a valuable tool to tell you when to get in and out of the market. Too many novice traders make the same mistake when it comes to taking profits and losses. They think in terms of their own circumstances, their bank accounts, their positions. The market doesn't know—and certainly doesn't care—about where you bought and sold a stock. Your market decisions, therefore, should be based on what the particular stock is likely to do in the future and not on your particular portfolio. By concentrating on the market and not your position, you are more likely to do the right thing.

This advice is easier said than followed. As a rule, you should ignore the advice of the crowd. Obviously, everyone wants to buy at the bottom and sell at the top. But you wouldn't know this by witnessing just about any bull or bear market. At market tops, the crowd is invariably enthusiastically bullish; at market bottoms, you can't give away stock. The inference to be drawn is simple: Don't follow the crowd. There is ample statistical evidence that the crowd is always wrong at the major turns in the market.

If investing were as easy as it looks to most people, everyone would be rich. But the facts demonstrate that enormous sums of money are lost every year because of the ignorance of average, everyday investors and, on a somewhat larger scale, by their cousins, the portfolio managers, who insist on doing what they think of as the right thing and end up losing fortunes in the process.

There are a lot of explanations for these losses, but the simplest one is human nature. We tend to be both greedy and fearful, regardless of our financial circumstances. There are times when it pays to be one or the other, but in general our emotions tend to get the best of us. For this reason, a detached analytical approach works best for buying and selling stocks.

THE MOST RELIABLE CHART PATTERNS

In seeking a reliable chart pattern, chart analysts typically look to what worked best in the past. When they find such a pattern, they look for a similar configuration in analyzing potential stocks to buy. As a rule, this propensity to identify tried-and-true patterns creates a sort of self-fulfilling occurrence: Because a stock generates a bullish pattern, buyers rush in, and the stock rises. Therefore, if a pattern proves profitable, investors attempt to recreate the same model again. They do this until they begin to lose money and then begin to look for another pattern. While there are no sure-thing patterns, there are commonly accepted ones that routinely appear on price charts. As a novice chartist, you will want to become familiar with the following widely watched chart patterns.

The Head and Shoulders

One of the most reliable of all patterns, the head and shoulders, appears, as the name suggests, as two well-defined shoulders with an extended head on the charts. Chartists also attempt to identify the neckline, which runs under the shoulders. This neckline must be penetrated for the move to begin. Occasionally, the market breaks and returns to the neckline prior to the real move occurring—the so-called return move. As a reversal pattern, the head and shoulders can signal a top or a bottom. The bottom reversal pattern has the head pointing down, and the top reversal pattern has the head pointing upright. With a little experience, these patterns are easy to spot. As a general rule, a breakout from the neckline carries the same distance as the distance between the top of the head and the neckline. The time to start monitoring the head-and-shoulders pattern is when it is two-thirds formed—after the completion of the head. Once the second shoulder is formed, it is simply a matter of buying or selling the breakout or waiting for the return move to the neckline to place your position. Because most low-priced stocks are better buying candidates than selling candidates, you are probably better off looking for a head-and-shoulders bottom as opposed to a top.

The Saucer Bottom

This is a compelling bottom pattern because it takes a long time to form and is easy to spot. In the saucer formation, prices trade essentially sideways for a prolonged period, creating a gentle scoop like a soup dish. Finally, prior to the breakout, the pattern is characterized by a handle formation. The breakout from the handle is usually powerful. Saucer bottoms require the investor to be patient. This pattern is also known as a cup and handle.

Rising and Falling Wedges

These tend to be continuation patterns, way stations where prices hesitate before resuming the prior trend. Formed in the shape of a wedge, these continuation patterns give investors time to exit profitable positions or initiate new positions before the inevitable upward or downward trend continues.

Ascending, Descending, and Symmetrical Triangles

The best way to characterize triangles is to say that they become tightly wound in advance of the breakout. In a triangle, prices are gyrating back and forth in tighter and tighter ranges as the apex is approached. At the apex, prices break out higher or lower, depending on which pattern is occurring. In the ascending triangle, prices rise up to the resistance as they approach the apex; in the descending triangle, prices trade near the support prior to breaking down. In the symmetrical triangle, prices trade in a narrow range near the middle of the triangle as they approach the apex. The breakout signals the direction of the move.

Double and Triple Bottoms and Tops

These can be the most significant of all chart patterns. A double bottom occurs when prices trade to a key support level twice. They then bounce off that level. The reverse is true of a double top, where prices bounce down from a resistance level. Triple tops and bottoms are even more important. The rule is that on the third attempt to penetrate a support or a resistance, the price must go. Otherwise, if the support or resistance holds, prices go in the opposite direction.

Gaps

Gaps, which we briefly discussed in connection with breakouts, can be a powerful chart pattern. Used by so-called momentum investors, who rely on high-volume breakouts to pinpoint opportunities, gaps can signal when a stock is poised to run or, in some instances, when a price move is exhausted. The particular stage of the price move is reflected in the names given to gaps, such as breakaway, continuation, and exhaustion gaps. In each of these gaps, the momentum players are typically behind the moves. But you must be careful if you are planning to utilize the gap as a justification for taking a position. Whereas the breakaway gap is often a legitimate buy signal, the exhaustion gap, as the name suggests, can be quite the opposite.

THE REAL VALUE OF TECHNICAL ANALYSIS

No doubt you have heard of the K.I.S.S. principle, namely, "Keep it simple, stupid." Technical analysis is steeped in arcane language that might cause the MBA's heart to beat faster but leaves the average guy feeling clueless.

To use another cliché, this isn't rocket science. Just the name alone brings to mind people in white coats holding clipboards. You don't need a Ph.D. to understand stock analysis, only an open mind to think a step in front of the crowd. This is not to minimize the challenge of successful stock selection. It can be difficult and trying. But the first principles concentrate on two things: when to buy a stock and when to sell a stock. Everything else is frivolous.

You already know the answer to both questions. The time to buy a stock is when it is low, and the time to sell it is when it is high, preferably at the top, which, as we all know, is easier said than done. We've already mentioned that quite a few investors do the very opposite despite their stated intention of making money in their investment activities. The reason so many individuals emerge as losers in the market is that they fail to understand what is going on. They fail to see the obvious things, such as insiders unloading their shares following rosy earnings and guidance reports. They fail to see why the company never measures up to its expectations. They fail to see through the Enron-type schemes, when fraud is rampant in the company but the stock price soldiers on higher. It is not that these individual investors want to be taken to the cleaners. On the contrary, they simply want to believe. As you will soon see, all this is unnecessary if you simply learn to correctly read the market.

The successful study of technical analysis is the antidote to this market blindness. Much of what passes for technical analysis, however, only serves to blur the situation, by stressing esoteric oscillators, meaningless stochastic numbers, Fibonacci points, cardinal squares, and the like. The pertinent question that technical analysis needs to answer is far less complicated: Where is my stock going and when is it going to get there?

The experts can sit around and argue all they want about the technical weakness or strength of a given market or security. The only real value to technical—or, for that matter, fundamental—analysis is whether it can make money for the investor. Again, the salvation of the strategy is its predictive abilities. If you tell me to sell once the trendline is broken, chances are I'm selling into a crowd of sellers and getting a lousy fill. If you tell me to buy a breakout, I may indeed luck out and make money. But I may also buy the top if the breakout turns out to be false. Simply put, the conventional wisdom of technical analysis is woefully inadequate to my needs.

Now for the good news: What if I told you that technical analysis can tell you not only where a market is going but when it is likely to get there? Moreover, it can tell you in advance of the crowd. Depending on your time frame, technical analysis can tell you when a market will peak or bottom within a few days, a few hours, or even a few minutes. The benefit is that you will be selling into strength and buying into weakness. This, after all, was the original intention of the millions of market participants who truly want to make money in the market.

We've mentioned that this type of technical analysis is *predictive*, putting you ahead of the crowd. But it is also *reactive* because it has to be. It enables you to read the price action before the underlying move is known. The signals won't always prove profitable, of course. Nothing works all the time. But you will know whether you are right or wrong because you have a virtual road map of what should occur when you use this method.

TIME AND PRICE

The time and price method of technical analysis pinpoints where a stock should trade in the future and when it should get there. The explanation of time and price is simple. Trends—uptrends or downtrends—occur in two-leg segments. The segments tend to be identical in time and price. The trends may be observable over many months or even within a single morning's trading session. Accordingly, you may have an uptrend in the morning and a downtrend in the afternoon. While this information is important to day traders, the longer-term trader will, no doubt, long for a more substantial run.

How do you tell if a market will run? Simple. You watch it. The market for a given stock will tell you very clearly. It will run up or down. If it stays sideways (consolidating), leave it alone. Does that mean you lose part of the move? Absolutely. You allow the market to tell you where it wants to go. That's the first rule.

Let's say you have a universe of 25 or 30 low-priced stocks, all trading under $7. You can program your computer to tell you which stocks gained more than 5 to 10 percent in value. And to further pinpoint the best ones, you can tell the computer to read out the ones that traded at more than 50 percent of their normal volume. Now, you have stocks in play in terms of both price and volume.

The next step: Watch the stocks that are moving. That's right, watch them, but don't buy them. Anyone can rush in and buy the top. That's strictly for amateurs. The price direction—we'll assume they moved up—tells you whether you want to be a buyer or a seller. Now you know that you want to buy XYZ stock. But where would you want to buy it? It makes sense to wait at least until the stock stops advancing. What you are seeking is information—information concerning how sustained the move is and whether it can hold its gains. The stock may have been a one-day wonder. In this instance, the move is over, and you will want to leave it alone. Can you see how jumping on a surging stock can be a big mistake?

Because this notion of time and price is probably new to most readers, let me spell out the steps that must be taken to quickly analyze a stock.

Moreover, since time and price are two separate variables, let's take them one at a time. Here are the steps:

To determine the *price objective* for a stock:

1. **Find a stock that is already trending.** That's right, glance through a list of charts and find a stock that has already begun a move. Ignore stocks that are trending lower for right now, and concentrate on those that are rising.

2. **Measure the magnitude of the move from low to high.** You are looking for a single upward trend. Measure from the absolute low of a trend to the high of the trend. Make a note of this measurement. For example, let's say XYZ stock started the move from a low of $3.50 a share and increased in value to $5.00 a share. The distance is the difference, or $1.50. This then becomes the value of what is called the first leg of the trend.

3. **Wait for prices to consolidate.** This is the profit-taking phase when investors take profits on the first move up. This selling will inevitably send prices lower. Let's assume, for the sake of this illustration, that XYZ trades down as low as $4.50 a share, where the shares then stabilize.

4. **Measure the profit objective.** The profit objective is measured by taking the value of the first leg and adding it to the price where the stock consolidates (or churns sideways). This is also known as the equilibrium price. In our illustration, the profit objective, or sell point, would become $6.00 a share ($4.50 equilibrium + $1.50 value of first leg = $6.00 profit objective).

5. **Buy at the equilibrium price.** In our illustration, this is $4.50 a share.

6. **Place an order to sell at the profit objective.** Sell at $6.00 a share.

In a nutshell, this is all you need to do to determine where to buy and sell a stock by using price measurements. Now, let's turn to the notion of time.

Here are the rules for determining the *timing* of the trade, when the stock should trade at the price objective:

- **Measure the number of days in the first leg.** How many trading days did it take for the first leg to be completed? In our illustration, when XYZ rose from $1.50 to $5.00 on the first leg, let's say the entire move took just three days from bottom to top.

- **Add the number of days in the first leg to the breakout day from the consolidation.** Using the breakout day as day 1, count ahead the number of days in the first leg: day 1, day 2, day 3, and so on. In this illustration, day 3 would be the target sell day.

You now have both price and time objectives. You know you want to sell XYZ at a price of $6.00 a share on the third day up from the breakout from the consolidation. This is the essence of time and price.

MOMENTUM

Momentum players, like time and price analysts, look for clear-cut signals in the market. For the momentum trader, volume is the key. A market rising on high volume is the momentum investor's dream play. As a market powers higher, it goes through phases. These are reflected in the names given to the various gaps that appear on the chart, such as the breakaway, continuation, and exhaustion gaps. In each of these gaps, the momentum players are behind the moves. But you must be careful if you are planning to jump aboard late in the trend.

As a market moves higher, the degree of speculative activity tends to increase. Intelligent momentum players understand that they must be present in the accumulation phase of the move (which, naturally, occurs at the beginning). They then use the distribution phase as an opportunity to sell. Uninformed buyers always exist at the top. Their buying drives prices to unrealistic heights.

During the momentum phase, prices continue to move up. What signals the end of the move is the rate at which prices rise. This reflects the quality of the buying as the market reaches its heights. This buying goes through distinctive phases as prices rise. First is the accumulation phase, followed by the markup, speculation, and distribution phases.

Momentum traders are characterized by the speed with which they move in and out of the market. They look for stocks that have fast, predictable high-percent gains. When they identify a candidate, they jump on the stock immediately. And they are quick to take profits and leave in search of another momentum play. Needless to say, those Johnny-come-lately traders who seek momentum plays in the distribution phase are like moths to the flame. They are drawn in and then quickly flame out. Rare is the stock, no matter how strong the underlying fundamentals, that can bear up under sustained speculative activity.

As you can see, the momentum player's horizon is short. It could be as short as an hour or as long as 10 days. So don't try to turn a momentum trade into a long-term investment. If you are going to profit from this pattern, you must follow the actions of the smart money.

Finally, while gaps have been mentioned as one characteristic of the momentum pattern, they do not always occur. Accordingly, you must not insist on a gap occurring to signal a momentum trade.

A WORD ABOUT SHORT SELLERS AND HOW THEY IMPACT A STOCK'S PRICE

Because we are primarily interested in purchasing low-priced stocks, we will stress the buying side of the buy/sell equation as our entry trade. The selling is related primarily to getting out of acquired positions. *Short selling* is a perfectly legitimate market strategy, but it presents problems when you are talking about low-priced stocks. One is that most brokerage houses won't allow their clients to enter into short positions in stocks trading under $5 a share. Another is the presence of a very real risk when one is selling short. You absolutely must cover, or buy back, your short positions, regardless of the cost of the stock. So if you short a stock selling at $9 a share and it promptly rises to, let's say, $18 a share, you just lost $9 a share, the maximum amount you stood to earn on the short position. Moreover, there's no telling where a stock will rise to. The downside, of course, is zero. So when you sell short, your profits are limited, and your potential losses are unlimited.

Ironically, short sellers provide a hidden value to the buyers of stocks. Because they must cover any short positions, they create a tremendous buying power in the event that prices rise. In a case of a stock breaking out to higher ground, the short sellers must join the new buyers entering the market as momentum players and other interested buyers. Their buying adds fuel to the bullish fire. This is all to the advantage of the initial stock buyers who purchased lower down. In addition, their buying provides valuable liquidity (meaning you will have an eager buyer to sell to, should you want to take profits). If anything, you should be more concerned if there are not any short sellers in a security you are thinking of buying.

Then there is the psychological factor involved in shorting stocks. You are betting against someone's future. When a stock rises, everyone can make out: you as the investor, certainly your broker, the company, even the customers or clients who benefit from the company's products and services. Apart from bankruptcy attorneys, who profits when a stock falls apart? Even if you could readily sell short a stock selling for just 50 cents or a dollar, why run the risk? These stocks can—and do—double and triple overnight. That's why you want to buy them.

CHAPTER 3

Profitable Strategies

N o doubt after reading the chapter on technical analysis, you are eager to get started on identifying patterns and looking for stocks that are suitable buying candidates. This is understandable because finding and buying profitable stocks is a rewarding activity. But where should you start? Among hundreds of low-priced stocks, how do you find the best ones? One approach is to start with the basics and build upon simple strategies with more sophisticated filters as your understanding and knowledge of the market increases. We discussed some of the basic patterns in the prior chapter. Let's turn now to putting the theory into practice.

IDENTIFY SUPPORT

One place to begin your inquiry is to identify stocks that have been breaking down and have shown early signs of support. The notion of support is critical for buying low-priced shares because it places a floor under all your buying activities. If the support holds—as it should—you know the risks when you take a position. The support price serves to draw out buyers who perceive the support as a low, meaning the buyers accumulating at those levels will see to it that the floor holds.

In identifying support, you will find that you will want an abundance of evidence that the support indeed exists. A market that is free-falling will not have support. There may be a spike higher after a prolonged break. But this chart pattern is more likely to be driven by daredevils than by legitimate buyers of the stock who perceive value. Support takes time to be established.

Where do you begin? Look for a market that has driven prices down. With a few exceptions, stock prices tend to follow the overall market averages. When you have a market decline, therefore, many stocks share the same overall chart pattern. Prices break and go sideways for a period of time. Then the support is broken, and prices move to a lower level. At the end of the move, you have what is known as capitulation, when even the heartiest bulls give up and sell. If you can observe this pattern in a dispassionate manner, carefully awaiting your opportunity, you will find that bargains become truly plentiful.

Following the capitulation phase, stocks tend to meander mostly sideways, but also a little higher and a little lower. Again, this is not the time to jump into the market but rather a time to begin a serious analysis of what is truly going on. At this stage, an important transformation is taking place. The informed, smart money is patiently accumulating shares from the ill-informed investors who have given up. The overall gloom of the market is palpable, and the pundits claim that a financial Armageddon is on the horizon. This is the perfect scenario for finding a good low-priced stock.

Understand that there is not just one support level but many as a stock begins its rise. Stocks trade within consolidation zones prior to breaking out. As a stock reaches a new price level, a new support is created; buyers then step in and purchase shares as the stock's price trades near the support.

I am reminded of a story that was told to me by a friend who met a hedge fund manager on an airplane. The conversation invariably got around to stocks, and the fund manager was telling my friend how bullish she was on a given stock. By the end of the plane trip, my friend had decided to become a buyer of the stock. Yet, being conservative in nature, she had one last question.

"What should I do if the stock goes down?" she asked.

"Don't worry," replied the fund manager. "We won't let it."

The point is that the hedge fund has sufficient funds and belief to support the stock, single-handedly if necessary. Needless to say, the stock made a substantial move higher.

Now I'm not suggesting that you need a major market player to provide you with good information to trade profitably. You can learn to read the market on your own so that the support zones—where the smart money is accumulating shares—become readily apparent.

I recently experienced a similar situation in a stock I had been accumulating for more than two years. The stock, like the overall market averages, had been drifting lower for several months. Rather than panic, I saw this as a legitimate opportunity to buy additional shares. I ended up buying more than a half-million shares on the break to lower prices, averaging down. At the bottom, which proved to be the major support, the news was utter hopelessness. Investors were selling this stock for a fraction of what they had paid. You couldn't find a single bullish report on the stock. After creating a strong support at the bottom, the share prices slowly moved higher. The stock doubled in price in the past five months, and it is poised to move significantly higher on positive earnings and future guidance. This was indeed the classic turnaround story. Did I ever consider selling a single share at the bottom? Not a chance.

Outstanding opportunities, such as this one, do not present themselves every day, but you need to know how to spot them when they do. Ironically, the greatest opportunity sometimes exists where the outlook appears the darkest. One key to spotting them is learning to identify support.

Investors are often tempted to purchase shares at a long-term support, but even this tried-and-true strategy has its pitfalls. Look at the long-term chart of Ford Motor Company (F) in Figure 3.1. On no less than three separate occasions in recent years, Ford sold off under $15 a share. On each of those occasions, it found support and rallied. It seemed as if $15 would prove to be a long-term support for Ford shares. But then Ford stock fell to $7.98, and $15 suddenly became an overhead resistance rather than a support. Ford is now trading at $8.40 a share, well below its previous support.

FIGURE 3.1 Long-Term View of Ford Shares

Stocks rise in a stair-step fashion. So while you can have major support at one level, you can have intermediate support levels all the way up. In the case of the Ford illustration, the slip under $15 proved to be its undoing. With the prior long-term support gone, the shares meandered lower, later stabilizing just above $8.

In looking for major and intermediate support, scroll back on your chart for major support and resistance areas in the past. Unfilled gaps are a classic area for a stock to find support and resistance. The rule is that the gap will be filled, so if you have a gap that occurred five or six months ago and prices never traded within that gap area, look for support or resistance in that area. Going up, of course, the gap area signifies resistance; coming down, a gap provides support. It all depends where the prices are today vis-à-vis the gap areas on the chart.

The same could be said for 52-week highs and lows. The market has a way of remembering where these key support and resistance levels are. Moreover, stop orders tend to bunch around the 52-week highs and lows. As a result, you will find that the support and resistance are often penetrated by just 5 or 10 cents, creating new 52-week highs and lows.

Technical analysis is inexact. So when you buy on dips, the place to do the buying is at the support.

Another benefit of this approach is that it can minimize your risk. If you have the discipline to buy at or near the support and sell immediately if the support is broken, you are limiting your downside exposure. If you likewise have the discipline to allow the market to rise without taking small profits, you will be adhering to the classic market dictum to let your profits ride and cut your losses short. Unfortunately, too many investors do the very opposite.

THE RULE OF THREE

The rule of three refers to the number of times a support or resistance is tested prior to resuming a trend. On the third attempt, the support or resistance ought to be broken. If it isn't broken, look for prices to move in the opposite direction. If you look at a two-year chart for the Barnes Group Inc. (B) (Figure 3.2), you will see that the key support level was $24 a share. The support was tested three times over the two-year period. In each case, the support held. Following the third and final test, Barnes's share prices soared $10 a share higher. Several years back, Barnes had formed support at $19 a share. Following the third failed attempt to penetrate the support, Barnes made a dramatic price rise.

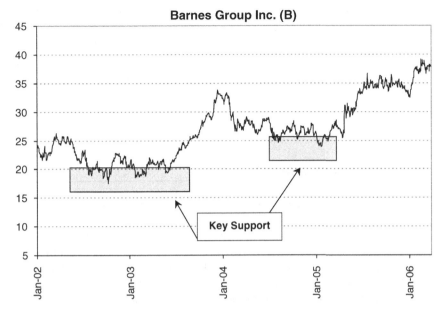

FIGURE 3.2　Two-Year Chart for the Barnes Group

You will see these three attempts to penetrate support or resistance in both major and intermediate support and resistance zones. Just remember: On the third attempt, it ought to go; if it doesn't, a price reversal is in store.

As you glance at price charts, try to identify the key support areas. I owned an oil services stock a couple of years ago that had a strong support at $6 a share. Despite an occasional break under that price, the stock stayed above $6 most of the time that I owned it. It later rallied above $10 a share, where I took profits. After I got out, it collapsed to—you guessed it!—$6 a share, the long-term major support.

There is an interesting story that relates to this oil services company. On one of the few occasions when it did break under $6 a share, it broke hard on a news event. Again, I treated the break as a buying opportunity and scooped up shares as it traded lower. Apparently, I wasn't alone. I later read that the company CEO bought several million shares on the one-day break to the bottom. Weeks later, the news turned bullish. That's when it soared above $10 a share. It is amazing how the fundamentals conveniently change to reflect the technical situation in a stock.

When you buy support, you are placing the odds in your favor. The point is not to panic if you get an occasional breaking of the support. If the support is legitimate, the stock price will bounce right back up, as it did in the illustration. Occasionally, you will see support that is broken on the way to lower prices. Obviously, this presents a problem. But as a rule, buy at the support in a beaten-down market and the profits will be yours. If the market is already trending higher, of course, step in and buy on dips to the intermediate support line. Remember, the market is never too high to buy and never too low to sell. If you follow these few simple rules, you won't regret it.

THE MOMENTUM PLAY

This strategy is not for the faint of heart, but the truth is, this is what often wins the game. This is an aggressive strategy that requires the investor to spend a lot of time on the sidelines waiting to strike when the iron is hot. Too often you will find that you are fully invested in stock A when the real opportunity exists in stock B. Your problem: Your money is all tied up in stock A. So if you want to be properly prepared, keep your powder dry.

There are two keys to capturing a powerful momentum play: price and volume. Because most moves are good for at least three days up (remember that the rule of three applies to a number of situations in the market), you must be willing to move quickly. A larger percentage gain is typically the first sign of a good momentum play. Moreover, this often manifests itself as a breakout. This, by the way, is why this strategy is so difficult to implement. Do you really want to be a buyer of a stock at a new high? A lot of investors find this psychologically hard to do. You also want high volume, far in excess of normal volume. The price percentage move and volume reading are relatively easy to identify. The hard part is pulling the trigger.

One way to capitalize on this strategy is to be prepared to take the position before a signal is given. You might track a given stock in anticipation of the momentum signal. Once the stock is in play, you must then, without hesitation, jump aboard the move. The time to spot a momentum trade is when the stock is coming down and the rate of descent begins to slow. At first, the price begins to consolidate; in this phase, the momentum is clearly changing from down to up. Next, the stock experiences accumulation by investors in search of an undervalued opportunity. Within the consolidation, look for a saucer pattern to form as prices begin to move sideways above the support. At this stage, the stock is poised to break out and move up on higher volume.

Ironically, a classic sign of a stock getting ready to move significantly higher is prices that drop to new lows. At this point, all hope for higher prices is lost. The last sell-stop has been hit, and the selling is palpable. Here you want to track the stock's behavior carefully. If indeed all hope is lost, you should have even lower prices. You may have just registered a 52-week low in the stock's price. But if there is a quick move up, with the stock perhaps closing at the top of its day's range, you have a classic reversal trade—a truly strong reversal that will attract momentum players. The point: A move that doesn't behave as anticipated signals a reversal.

In the recent case of Pelican Financial Inc. (PFI), the stock made a sustained move from the 52-week highs at $7.40 all the way down to the $5 area, which proved to be the bottom of the move. See Figure 3.3. After bottoming out, Pelican Financial made a clear-cut ascending triangle pattern on the chart. As it neared the apex of the triangle, momentum players lined up to jump on the stock as it powered higher. You have to identify these trades before they happen. Once the breakout occurs, the run to higher prices should proceed quickly.

The key to identifying this trade is the failure of the stock to fall below its prior 52-week low of $4.75 a share. The fact that the stock made a new low on the move (breaking the prior support) without follow-through on

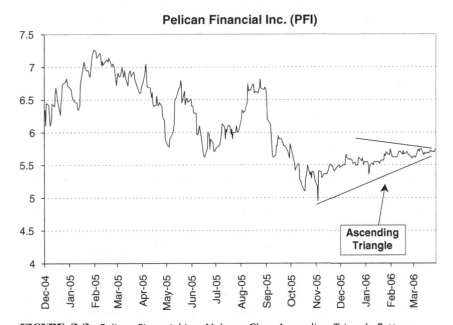

FIGURE 3.3   Pelican Financial Inc. Makes a Clear Ascending Triangle Pattern

the move was the key to the reversal. Next, the consolidation within the ascending triangle was the sign that the stock was getting ready to move substantially higher.

CONTRARY OPINION

Contrary opinion theorists will tell you that, at the major turns, the crowd is always wrong. This observation has been repeatedly proven by any number of stock market analysts who have studied the behavior of investors in major bull and bear markets. This is clearly a paradox (the definition of which is an apparent contradiction that is nevertheless somehow true). Why would the vast majority of investors be wrong at the major tops and bottoms? Humphrey Neill, who was once called the father of the contrary option, put it this way: "When everyone thinks alike, everyone is likely to be wrong" (*The Art of Contrary Opinion*, Fraser Publishing Company, 1954). Put another way, any one-sided thinking probably means the opposite will occur.

Consider the Internet bubble top in March 2000. Did you know anyone who thought that was a time to take profits? More likely, the average investor was buying stocks at the top, not selling them. Naturally, the reverse occurs at market bottoms. The bears are in control, and no one wants to purchase stocks in such an environment. Ironically, the winning strategy is to go against the crowd in selecting stocks. The natural tendency, however, is to go along with conventional wisdom. That's why stocks like Microsoft, Wal-Mart, and Disney routinely appear on the most active list. These clearly thriving companies are expected to continue to win in the market. Yet here a paradox exists. The mature company's stock is unlikely to make a strong percentage gain. The out-of-favor—not to mention unknown—company has a much better chance of registering impressive gains as it trades off its lows.

If you are going to win, you must seek out and find these little-known gems. Without attempting to highlight any given stock, here are some names of the *types* of stocks that qualify as little known and out of favor:

- **Covad Communications Group (DVW).** This San Jose, California–based nationwide provider of broadband voice and data communications recently got its shares listed on the American Stock Exchange. It is always a plus for a company to be listed on a major exchange as opposed to being just one of hundreds of companies listed as a bulletin board stock. This was a company that was trading near its 52-week low, prior to making a substantial rise. See Figure 3.4.

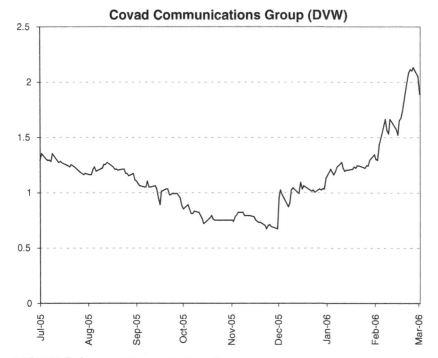

FIGURE 3.4 Covad Communications Group

- **Art Technology Group (ARTG).** Changing hands at just under a dollar a share, this Cambridge, Massachusetts–based software manufacturer recently reported a 41 percent year-over-year growth in revenues. See Figure 3.5.
- **HMS Holdings (HMSY).** This company is in the booming cost containment field for health-care payers and providers. The company consolidated midway between its 52-week high and low of $9 and $5.19, respectively. Having made a strong triple bottom at the $6 a share support level, HMS Holdings later climbed above 30. See Figure 3.6.

Dozens more examples could be considered little-known and out-of-favor stocks. They typically are priced low and trading at or near 52-week lows. These types of stocks offer some of the best opportunities for price appreciation. Some are in hot fields, and others are not. What they have in common is that they have yet to capture the attention of the Wall Street community.

Consider the case of JDS Uniphase (JDSU). Here was a $3 stock that had fallen by half to $1.50 a share. After forming strong support at that

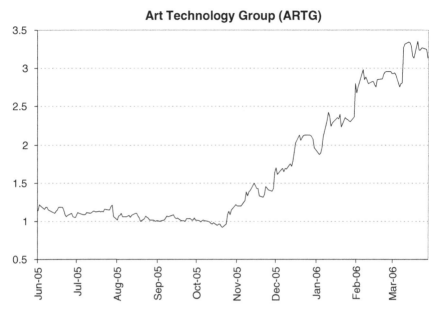

FIGURE 3.5 Art Technology Group

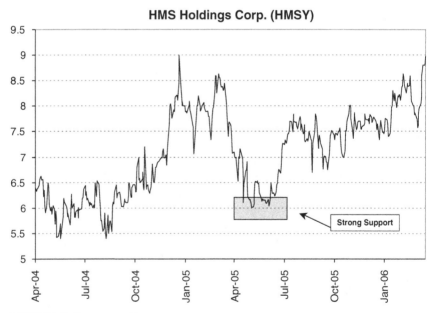

FIGURE 3.6 HMS Holdings

price, it was poised to move higher after months of being out of favor in the investment community. See Figure 3.7.

It is clear that everyone loves a winner when it comes to selecting stocks. The question is: Should they? Paradoxically, if you want to end up a winner, you should very often start out with a loser, or at least a winning stock that is currently out of favor. There may be a host of reasons why a stock is temporarily not popular. The company may be experiencing unsatisfactory developments such as poor earnings, a troubled management, or high start-up costs. But chances are these setbacks are temporary. Any return to profitability can quickly lead to a substantial increase in value for the company's shares.

As a contrarian, you want to buy when the crowd is selling. The bottom line is that the most impressive percentage gainers come from the ranks of the down and out, not the high-flying glamour stocks that so many investors find irresistible.

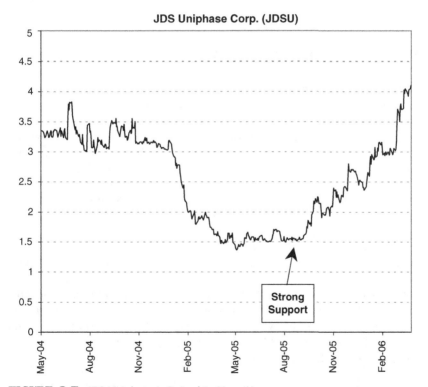

FIGURE 3.7 JDS Uniphase Is Poised to Move Up

IDENTIFY THE CORRECT PHASE
OF THE TREND

Stocks tend to rise and fall in predictable trends: the long-term (major), intermediate, and short-term (minor) trends. Ideally, we would always be capable of spotting the beginning of a major trend. But this is extremely difficult to do. Major bear and bull markets don't identify themselves, and market analysts are notoriously late in announcing the beginning of a new trend. Indeed, by the time that people start talking about a trend, that trend is probably due for a correction. For the investor, this can be a risky time to jump aboard a stock.

In our discussion on chart patterns, we have already mentioned how the chart analyst might look at long- or short-term patterns, depending on the chartist's particular time frame. The day trader, for instance, might be interested in a five-minute chart; the long-term trader, by contrast, might be content with a weekly chart. When discussing trends, you should understand that these time frames are also somewhat arbitrary as well.

A PERSONAL OBSERVATION

At the end of a recent quarter, I decided to pick three arbitrary time periods to analyze a stock that I owned. While I was well aware of what the stock had been doing, the charts provided graphic evidence that it was clearly trending higher. For the short term, I selected 5 days; for the intermediate, I looked at 30 days; and for the long term (which, granted, is relative), I picked 3 months, or 90 days. The results were clearly encouraging.

5-day gain	30-day gain	90-day gain
4 cents	16 cents	24 cents

These results tell me that the stock is in an uptrend over the short-, intermediate-, and long-term periods. Yet, if I were to go back over 90 days, I would find a completely different picture because the stock made a major low at that time. A second stock I owned, however, had just experienced a sharp selloff following a rise to new 52-week highs. I knew the short- and intermediate-term trends were down. Nevertheless, the long-term trend was clearly higher. This told me the recent break was temporary. Here are the numbers for the same period of time.

5-day gain (loss)	30-day gain (loss)	90-day gain
(11 cents)	(16 cents)	56 cents

As you can see, the three trends operate concurrently but not necessarily in unison. Looking back with 20-20 hindsight, I would have certainly sold the second stock if I had foreseen the sharp break coming. (I could have always bought it back at today's lower prices.) But on balance, I'm still bullish on the stock and am prepared to hold the stock for yet another penetration of the 52-week high, which could come on the next earnings announcement scheduled for 4 weeks from now.

Here again, the stock was in the doldrums at the beginning of the quarter. It had risen smartly, only to be hammered down when nervous speculators panicked. The break, in my opinion, had been purely technical. The fundamentals remained very bullish. In time, I fully expect to be vindicated by selling my shares at a much higher price.

In both of these examples, I was able to hold onto my shares during a declining market because I shared a belief that prices were indeed headed higher. Looking back, I can see that the bottom, like all bottoms, was characterized by wholesale selling by nervous investors and widespread accumulation by value-conscious investors looking to pick up a bargain at dirt-cheap prices. Now, three months down the road, I think we know who was able to capitalize on a good opportunity.

How do you know when the market is turning from bearish to bullish? The simple answer is that you don't. Indeed, the major trend is typically the last to be recognized. What is called for, then, is to make an educated guess. One strategy is to analyze the trends, starting with the shortest-term trend and then moving forward in time. You may have a bullish minor trend in a down market; then, with time, the intermediate-term trend may turn bullish; finally, you'll be in a full-blown bull market, and the pundits will be claiming, "I told you so."

What I'm talking about here is the classic "smoke coming out from under the door" syndrome, which must be recognized long before the fire department is summoned because the metaphorical house is on fire. In this instance, of course, to use the same metaphor, it is blazing good fortune that we are talking about.

The technical analyst, striving to capture a trend early in the move, tries to line up the ducks in a row by monitoring a host of technical indicators that may give early warning signals that a stock is seriously oversold. It should come as no surprise that the best gains are achieved when the stock's major trend is just beginning to change from down to up. To capture this trend, however, you often need to closely monitor the shortest-term trend, often the daily trend. There are two easy ways to find out which stocks are in play. One way is to check the daily most active list available in any local newspaper. The second is to check those stocks with the highest percentage gain. Typically, candidates for these lists are stocks that are breaking out of consolidation patterns based on a solid news story or strong earnings report. These stocks tend to dominate the headlines—at least while they are breaking out. They are often forgotten by the press once another story hits the headlines. But this can be a clue that a major trend is about to get under way. Be careful here, of course, lest a one-day wonder proves to be just that, and the stock retreats after fooling a lot of investors into buying the top. By now, we don't need to suggest that the move will be accompanied by high volume. Abnormally high volume is a component of virtually all stocks getting ready to generate substantial gains.

Although a stock may get some publicity when it first breaks out and starts to run, the real public interest doesn't come about until the stock has typically doubled and tripled in value. That's when you'll see a stock mentioned on CNBC or headlined in the press. One way to test this assertion is to track the stocks mentioned as good buy possibilities on the leading networks. Invariably, a glance at the stock's chart will reveal that the stock has already made a good run. I learned this publicity-follows-price philosophy firsthand several years ago after I bought 5,000 shares of Best Buy, Inc. (BBY) at $27 a share. At the time, Warren Buffett had just expressed an interest in the company and was accumulating shares, but many pundits thought the stock was overpriced. When the stock reached $37 a share, I sold my position, making a quick $50,000 profit. At the time, I was pleased with my successful investment. It didn't become a truly hot stock, however, until it traded over $50 a share. Now that the stock has traded at almost $80 a share, of course, the analysts are labeling it a strong buy! Where were they when I bought Best Buy at $27? (Note: Best Buy then issued a 3-for-2 stock split. Hence, the price is back in the $55 a share area. See Figure 3.8.)

As you can no doubt understand, the endorsement of a stock as a strong buy is often an excellent contrary indicator to sell. This is akin to the old story about an athlete's appearance on the cover of *Sports Illustrated* or a company becoming a headline story in the *Wall Street Journal*. Once you arrive in one of those prominent places, the path of least resistance is invariably down. The old saw about the trend being your friend is something I've never been comfortable with. How do you know the trend? And are we speaking of the short-, intermediate-, or long-term trend? Anyone can look at a price chart after a stock has dramatically risen and pronounce the trend as up. But does that mean it will continue higher from there?

Trend trading would be easy if prices, once under way, continued in the same direction. But there are those pesky drawdowns and profit-taking setbacks to which the market is often prone. The one thing you can count on when the inevitable profit-taking occurs is that many investors will invariably sell at the wrong time. This can truly be an opportunity for those with the foresight to see what is going on. One question you should ask

Best Buy Inc. (BBY)

3-for-2
Stock Split

FIGURE 3.8 Best Buy Issues a 3-for-2 Stock Split

yourself as events unfold is: Does this decline represent a change in the trend? Very often, you are looking at an opportunity to acquire additional shares at a discount price.

Rather than being blindsided when profit-taking hits the market, try to anticipate a decline following any substantial run-up in prices. Our price and time studies suggest that pullbacks are both healthy and predictable. A downward move on profit-taking or whatever is healthful because it sets up the scenario for higher prices again. It is predictable in the sense that nothing goes straight up forever, even if the stock is destined to trade at significantly higher levels. If you take a quick glance at Figure 3.9, a yearly chart of Qwest Communications (Q), you will readily see that the stock made a $2 a share gain, trending higher from approximately $2.75 a share to $4.75 a share, using rounded numbers. Since markets typically retrace 0.681 of their initial move, based on Fibonacci calculations, the support is approximately $1.25 off the high, or at $3.50. That's exactly where Qwest Communications shares stopped declining. The decline gave new buyers an opportunity to buy on this pullback for the anticipated move. It recently made a new 52-week high above $10 a share.

The trend can be your friend—if you know what you are doing.

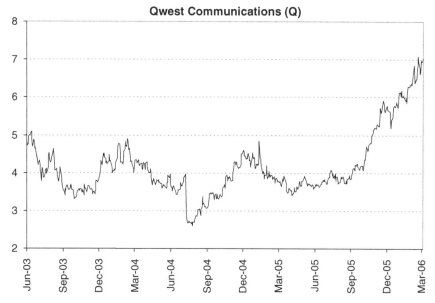

FIGURE 3.9 Qwest Communications

FINDING GOLD AMID THE DROSS

Nothing surprises me about the market anymore. I've experienced so many instances where out-of-favor stocks became legitimate highfliers and Wall Street darlings tanked and fell to earth that my only response is: What else is new? I once owned stock in a highly touted cellular phone company that proved to be the second worst performer on the Nasdaq for an entire year, beating out more than 3,300 other stocks for that dubious distinction. As the stock began its relentless move from above $10 a share to zero, the management issued statement after statement above the viability of the company, and stock analysts routinely took the time to address management in the company's conference calls. What we were listening to was, of course, nothing more than a scam. In the end, the patient couldn't be saved.

Experiences like these provide a powerful incentive to never let this kind of mendacity influence our investment decisions ever again. Yet any honest appraisal of our investment activities suggests an element of luck persists. The problem is that too often our perceptions are clouded by the immediate past. Several years ago, I inherited a small amount of money ($18,000 to be exact) that I wanted to put to work in the stock market. I bought stock in a small health-care provider and pretty much forgot about the investment because its primary price trajectory was sideways. Then one morning I was watching CNBC, which reported that shares in my modest health-care provider were halted.

I promptly picked up the phone and called my brokerage house, fearing the worst.

"What's going on with XYZ?" I asked the phone clerk. "I understand that trading has been halted. Not a bankruptcy situation, I hope."

He was typing in the symbol on his computer.

"No, sir. Good news. It looks like a takeover bid."

"In that case, sell it at the market when it opens up," I told him.

Overnight, my $18,000 investment had grown to $50,000! I'd been the recipient of some extraordinary good luck. I later used the money to buy a brand-new Porsche for cash.

As you can see, a person can do all the right things and be wrong. Conversely, you can do the wrong things and be right. Luck? Maybe. But I'm more inclined to believe that we make the luck we deserve. In the end, everything is always hard-won. If you allow yourself to put yourself in a position to win, you will invariably get your share of the breaks and good fortune. Years ago, I worked for a guy who used to say, "We are doing all the right things." He meant, of course, taking care of clients, seeking out new clients, and building the business step by step. He was enormously successful.

When it comes to investing in securities, you must do the same thing. Not every stock will prove to be a winner. That's a given. But if you keep taking the proper steps, you will find your share of the winners.

We've mentioned that when prospecting for low-priced shares, everyone loves a winner. But the results suggest that focusing only on proven winners is a mistake. Undervalued companies rarely appear in the winners column. You are more likely to find a bargain in the columns listing those issues making new 52-week lows. Stocks tend to be cyclical in nature. So today's percentage winner is unlikely to duplicate its achievements in the coming months. Here again, contrary opinion theory proves helpful. To illustrate how an out-of-favor security might be tomorrow's winner, look at baseball statistics. When the New York Yankees recently went into a serious slump and fell back in the standings, Yankee haters throughout the country were delighted. But the Yankees were too strong a team to stay down on the deck for long. They put together an impressive winning streak and climbed back out of the cellar. The general rule is that any aberration away from the norm (higher or lower) will see a movement back to the center. This applies to both baseball statistics and stocks alike. Accordingly, stocks that have fallen out of favor should be seen as likely candidates for price appreciation.

Leading business publications, such as *Fortune*, *Forbes*, *Investors' Business Daily*, and *Barron's*, are forever printing lists of both highly admired and out-of-favor companies that make for interesting reading. The so-called darlings of the Street are highly hyped while the dogs are routinely trashed. It is not an accident that the same stocks appear in the most active list of the newspaper every day. These are the stocks that enjoy the widest participation. Investors maintain a love affair with these stocks that regularly get front-paged in the financial press. Lucent, Disney, Microsoft, Wal-Mart, and even Motorola probably get more ink than the bottom 500 stocks combined. What is amazing is how often these very same stocks perform in a lackluster fashion. This makes a person wonder what investors are really after. *Fortune* is quick to highlight its "Top Gun" alongside its "Top Dog," and you'd think the former stood head and shoulders above the latter. But the statistics suggest the very opposite. It seems that popularity is not always a gauge of a security's future price performance.

To the stock technician, price is the final arbiter of a stock's success. The analysts can hype a stock and perhaps get a short-lived rally going. But in the end, the company must perform. And that performance or lack of performance will surely be reflected in the stock's price.

The dilemma for the investor is how to differentiate the truly hopeless companies—the WorldComs and Enrons—from the down-and-out companies that may be ready to get off the mat and fight another day. It is no secret that even bankruptcy candidates have become highfliers once management tackled the company's problems head-on. We all know the Penn Central story. Even some of the airlines have been able to weather the bankruptcy storm and surface as viable companies. Firms that successfully emerge from bankruptcy can have a bright future. On the other hand, it is not an accident that Bernard Ebbers was given a 25-year prison sentence.

Sometimes it only takes a single bad earnings report to send a stock plummeting. I've ridden through enough surprises to understand that investors are a notoriously disloyal lot. They want consistent strong earnings, lest they jump ship. And their panicked selling following an unfavorable report only serves to highlight the insanity of their behavior. The company remains in business. Given sufficient time, the earnings invariably improve—and, quite often, the stock price rises *above* its previous high.

Once again, the winners are the shareholders who either hold on during the break or those new buyers who step in and support the stock.

Finally, we can all understand why a stock goes down on bad news—but what about the "buy the rumor, sell the news" syndrome that causes a stock to plummet on good news? This bizarre phenomenon occurs when investors' expectations are out of line with reality. No company can be expected to consistently outperform itself, any more than a sixth-grader should be proficient at mastering medical school. If there was ever a time when opportunity presents itself, it is when a company registers strong earnings and tumbles in price. Over the years, I've wit nessed a number of situations where management had engineered a truly phenomenal turnaround, only to see the company's share prices decline because the earnings were not robust enough to meet investors' heightened expectations. Clearly, there is one sure antidote to this particular market malaise—buy the stock!

I've mentioned the notion of creating your own luck in the market. By that, I mean doing the things that set you up for possible good fortune. My personal approach is to focus on a few issues and watch them closely. One often hears, "Don't put all your eggs in one basket." But that's exactly what I'm suggesting here. That's because large positions in small stocks can return enormous profits. When you are truly diversified, as the pundits suggest, you are frequently caught unaware, watching the wrong stocks when you should have been concentrating on a handful of issues. Can this approach, of putting all your eggs in one basket and watching them carefully, go awry? You bet. You can pick the wrong stocks. But by concentrating on a handful of issues, you are likely to maintain a heightened awareness of the nuances of the stock you are holding, thereby smoothing the way for substantial profit.

THE BOTTOM REVERSAL

We all want to buy the bottom when the downtrend comes to an end. After the fact, this is typically an easy spot to identify. But while it is taking place, the bottom is often hard to find. The first step in finding a bottom is to anticipate just such a pattern. The outlook for the stock will be gloomy, and the selling, more often than not, will be overwhelming. So if you want to run a check on your emotions, a good signal that a bottom is near is the feeling that you would never want to buy the stock. Bearish sentiment is always strongest at the bottom. At the point where no one wants the stock, you probably want to step in and be a buyer.

Over the years, I've made many attempts to buy bottoms. That's because I'm a firm believer in averaging down (buying more when the stock declines). More often than not, the stock you are buying isn't going to zero—although, in some cases, the stock will. So you must be careful. Should you find yourself getting overly aggressive and persistent on buying breaks, you may be setting yourself up for ruin. You want to be aggressive but not destructive. There's an old saying in the financial markets that goes: "I bought the first break, I bought the second break, I *was* the third break!" This means that you caused the panic that drove the market to new lows. This is an obvious exaggeration, but it makes the point.

Markets get overdone—at both the top and the bottom. A friend of mine, in speaking of the anticipation of a bottom pattern, put it this way: "This market won't go up," he explained, "until every last long is killed." Long, of course, refers to people who were buyers of the stock. This is the kind of perverse sentiment that exists throughout the market. In order for the market to rise, it must first go down. This is why the reverse of what is anticipated often occurs. For instance, investors anticipate positive earnings. So they do the logical thing: They bid the stock higher. The earnings are released as anticipated, and the stock breaks like a rock. Or investors feel certain that a lowering of interest rates by the Fed will provide a boost to stock prices. The rates are lowered, and stock prices fall apart. They are many, many examples of the sheer perversity of the market. Remember the words of contrarian guru Humphrey Neill: "If everybody thinks alike, everybody is likely to be wrong!"

At the bottom of any market, you can bet that everyone is wrong. If they were right about the market, they would be busy buying the stock as opposed to selling it. Not long ago, when one of the companies that I own was making a significant bottoming action, I monitored the stock's chat room on Yahoo Finance. The comments were clearly one-sided: "That's it. I'm out of here. I'll never buy this stock ever again." "This company is headed for delisting and bankruptcy." "Management lied to us again." "Better opportunities elsewhere." "This stock will never go up." Within three months, the stock had doubled in value. The sheer negativity of the sentiment actually made me feel confident because I realized how infrequently the crowd is correct at the major turns. Indeed, the point to be worried is when you find yourself agreeing with the majority.

As you can see, buying and selling correctly is a lonely process. In my days as a floor trader, I would find people aimlessly wandering around the trading floor looking for someone to talk to. "These bonds have to go up, right?" they would demand. This is called talking your position, a sure sign that they were long bonds but had lost hope. They were looking for confirmation that they were on the right side of the market.

On a chart, you can find a graphic representation of this loss of hope. That's where you see new lows occurring day after day and then, finally, one last killer move to the downside! That is the sign that the move is over. A confirmation of the move is the closing price. If the stock can close on its high after a sharp run to new low ground, you have what is known in technical analysis as a key reversal day. That's the sign to start buying with both hands! You must do this with the knowledge that the final low has been established. That low must hold. And you must move quickly because it won't be long before an explosive rally will occur, typically driven by short sellers who are now panicky buyers in a rallying market.

If you have been tracking your stock with a chart and trendlines, you will notice that the down trendline has been broken as prices begin to trade higher. The volume on the bottom day typically doubles or even triples normal daily volume. The stock cannot make such a dramatic move within a vacuum.

Once the tide has turned and the trend has switched from lower to higher, you must then begin to execute your buying plan, looking for dips to add to your position. The new trend is now under way.

In looking back on such a reversal, you will note three things: one, the total absence of bullish sentiment just prior to the bottom; two, the pickup in volume as the stock first plummets and then reverses; and, three, the courage required to buy when the crowd is mindlessly selling. If you are able to accomplish such a feat, you deserve your hard-won profits.

If you want to see a stock that is setting up a buying opportunity, take a look at Citigroup (C). Citigroup, with a 52-week range of approximately $50 and $45 in round numbers, is trading near its lows. If the 52-week low holds, the stock will inevitably reverse. See Figure 3.10.

As the stock trades higher, the new buying will certainly mean the down move is over. At last glance, Citigroup was trading at $48.41 a share.

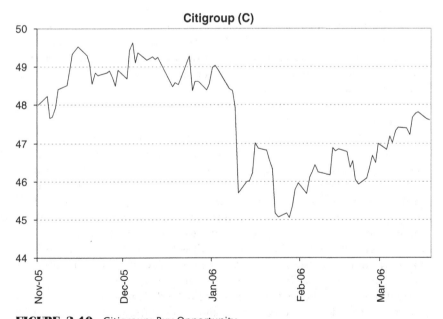

FIGURE 3.10 Citigroup: Buy Opportunity

AGGRESSIVE BUYING

It is not enough to be able to pinpoint trends in the market unless you are willing to capitalize on those trends by being an intelligent and aggressive buyer. There are times to be cautious in your buying—what I called test-the-waters buying—when you simply want information as opposed to a making-money position. But the real art is knowing when and where to buy. As we've discussed, the breakout is a classic opportunity in any stock that is about to trend from one trading level to another. A second and third opportunity then will become apparent as the initial trend begins to slow as a result of profit-taking. This selling inevitably drives prices lower. This pullback is where you want to buy. After three well-timed entries (remember the rule of three), you are pretty much ready to sit back and enjoy the ride to higher prices.

There will come a time, of course, when it is too late in the trend to continue buying. At this stage, it is okay to continue to hold the shares you already possess. But don't add to your position, because the risk/reward equation definitely begins to turn against buyers and in favor of sellers as prices move higher. If, for some reason, you failed to buy on the breakout or subsequent pullbacks, do *not* attempt to chase the market higher as a Johnny-come-lately. These are invariably desperation buys that can be extremely risky.

If you find yourself averaging—that is, buying more as the stock declines in prices—you must adhere to the rule of three. Within a consolidation range, this can be an effective means of lowering your overall purchase price. After three attempts to buy at lower prices, however, the stock ought to resume its upward momentum. If it doesn't, you may have made a serious miscalculation. This will require a decision on your part whether to continue to hold the position.

We've discussed the notion of buying the breakout and how a strategy of buying new highs can get you aboard a powerful and explosive move. The countermove strategy, however, is a bit more sophisticated because now you are fading—or trading against—the intermediate move, which is clearly lower. The maximum countermovement that you want a stock to experience is never more than 0.618 (or approximately 60 percent) of the initial move. By definition, when buying by using this strategy, you want a strong, clearly identified trend higher. It is the countermove down from that uptrend that presents the buying opportunity. Moreover, it is important to understand that the 0.618 retracement benchmark is the *maximum* amount of price adversity you want to withstand. At this point, it is important to point out the paradox: A small move down from the highs is a good buy, but a large move down from the highs is a bad buy. In other words, it is better to buy the stock higher than lower within the consolidation. The reasoning behind this is that stocks trade within definite technical patterns. Once they lose too much ground, the bulls get nervous and turn into bears—and, if the downward trend persists, pretty soon the whole world wants to sell. Witness any sharp break in the market, and you will see the truth of this statement.

A pullback to any prior support or trendline is also a sensible place to add to your position, given the parameters we just discussed. Technical analysts are always trying to play the percentages when they invest their money in the stock market. They want to minimize risk by buying as close to the bottom of the intermediate move as possible. Because the support levels and trendlines and, finally, the 0.618 Fibonacci retracement level is where prices are expected to stop declining, that's where the bulk of the buying will be concentrated. Violations of any of these significant levels could, of course, suggest that all bets are off. That's when you will experience a run to the exits—and sharply lower prices.

Different stocks tend to trade in different patterns. That's another argument why you should confine your trading activities to just a handful of issues. You want to become comfortable with your stocks' price swings. Assuming you know your stocks and how they behave in reaction to news events, you won't be shaken out of the market on a normal swing that is unfamiliar to you. For example, I own a stock that has relatively few shares available to the public. Even inconsequential news events can move the stock significantly higher or lower. Knowing this, I'm not concerned with negative swings because I understand it will snap back just as quickly when good news hits the market.

Nevertheless, you must be prepared for a time when a stock ceases to trade as its old self and begins to defy rhyme and reason. This will occasionally happen to highly speculative stocks that suddenly attract a wide following. The price swings may become unrealistic. Unfortunately, this often happens when the stock is nearing the top. That's when the upswings can be dramatic and the investor becomes euphoric. Beware of this feeling. It means disaster is lurking just around the bend. When you can't believe the money you are making in the stock market, you are inevitably about to get your comeuppance. Sell the stock at the market and take the profits; the end is near.

One sign that a stock is entering the so-called blow-off stage is when its self-correcting pattern ceases to exist. The rallies are no longer burdened by profit-taking, as more and more buyers purchase the highs—only to see the stock surge still higher. This then becomes a self-fulfilling prophecy. After the final buyer purchases the high, there is only one way the price can go, which is down. Any stock that runs just straight up, without hesitation, is creating a situation that will inevitably be to the detriment of the buyers who arrived late in the game. Investors who buy in the final stages of a blow-off top are not aggressive buyers, but reckless buyers. The market is said to trade on a continuum between fear and greed. This pattern occurs when the market is overwhelmingly characterized by greed. There is an old saying: "Bulls make money, bears make money. But pigs get slaughtered."

WHEN TO CUT AND RUN

Not all your stock purchases will prove profitable. So don't expect to make money on every trade. The idea is to have the profits outweigh the losses, but you wouldn't know this by observing the trading practices of many investors. Rather than letting their profits ride, they tend to hold on to the losers and take quick, small profits in the winning issues. I am reminded of the mindlessness of some public traders every year when I have my annual physical. My physician, who fancies himself as an investor, is always telling me, "You won't go broke taking a profit." But I want to say, "Doctor, stick to medicine." You surely will go broke taking a profit if you allow the losses to mount on losing trades and let the good opportunities get away by taking small profits. I know that I can make a lot of money if I have as many as twenty small losses for every winner—*if* the single winning investment is large enough to offset the losses. Fortunately, this is not my win/loss ratio. But the point is an important one. The ratio of winners to losers is unimportant; the important statistic is the relative *size* of the winners and losers.

With so much emphasis put on winning in our popular culture, it always amazes me how unsophisticated investors are when it comes to owning up to defeat. To listen to all the analysts on CNBC, you get the impression that no one ever loses money. Moreover, I am puzzled by these new disclosure rules that require analysts to say whether they own the stock. To me, owning the stock is an endorsement of being willing to put your money where your mouth is. I want the analyst to own the stock. Indeed, if the stock is such a great buy, why should an investor trust an analyst who hasn't bought the stock? Perhaps the commentator is praising the stock because the analyst's brokerage house wants to unload the shares to an unsuspecting public.

It should come as no surprise that most investors enter the market with no thought to the downside of the transaction. What if they are wrong? Do they have an exit plan? Buying stocks in general is risky, but low-priced stocks can be especially hazardous because of the many imponderables associated with speculation in these high-risk issues. It is a generally accepted tenet in the investment world that reward is commensurate with risk. No matter how successful you are, you simply cannot eliminate the risk. So why not do the sensible thing and embrace the risk? Every time I buy one of these little gems I understand that I might be making a big mistake. Indeed, a number of them have proven to be just that. But it doesn't mean I'm frightened of the risk. The idea is to accept and manage the risk.

Too often novice traders approach the notion of risk management in terms of their own financial circumstances. This is definitely the wrong way to deal with risk. The risk has nothing to do with the size of your pocketbook and everything to do with the price action of the underlying security you are buying and selling. The time to get out with a loss is when the investment no longer makes sense. The stock may have broken a support area or violated a trendline; in other words, the technical situation has changed. This is far different from getting out because you bought too high and now this temporary setback has eaten into your equity. The stock doesn't know that you own it. The market has nothing personal against you. Another way to look at this problem is to think in terms of the stock's chances for price advancement versus your bottom line, the money. The rule is: Don't think about the money; think about the position.

As you move across the continuum from total novice investor to professional investor, you will find that the more sophisticated players are extremely risk-conscious. The professional investor won't think twice about taking at least some profits when a stock doubles in price. The standard rule is to take off half the position at that stage, leaving the rest for additional profit if the market continues to advance. But novice traders treat risk in a far more cavalier fashion. They see good fortune as their birthright and become both confident and arrogant as their fortunes improve. Simply put, the professional understands the risks; the novice does not. This is why novice investors are continually caught up in disasters such as the recent Internet bubble. The professionals see this as the aberration that it was and move on. The novice investors are still bemoaning their fate. There's a little-known Arabic saying that goes: "Take what you want and pay for it." It goes to the heart of the notion of responsibility that is called for in attempting any high-risk venture, whether it be investing in securities or sailing around the world.

Part of the responsibility of trading stocks in a sensible manner is to manage the risk. Conventional wisdom dictates that positions should be protected by stop-loss orders. This is fine in theory, but the reality is often far different. A stop-loss order to sell a stock at a certain price becomes a market order once it is hit. This means you will be sold out of your position at some price. Given market conditions, the execution price could be far away from the initial stop price. It all depends on where the executing broker finds a buyer for your shares. Because stops are often bunched together in predictable places—under the 52-week lows, just below a support level or a trendline—they are easy to run by seasoned professionals who understand that the market will take on a life of its own once the stops are triggered. Specifically, your selling will generate additional selling as the market is offered down. This flurry of selling will cause the market, at least momentarily, to decline. At this point, the professionals, who began the foray into the stops, will step in and buy—after you have sold to them at the lows. The next move is up and your stock is off to the races—without you aboard. If you don't think this perfectly legal practice occurs, ask yourself why you sold shares at the low of the day that last time your stops were hit. Stop-running is a routine maneuver among market professionals. It is also known as *lowballing* and *highballing*, depending on where the stops are placed and the general direction of the market.

Then there is that pesky problem of so-called front running—a not-so-legal but nevertheless cherished practice. Front running occurs when a market insider, such as a floor specialist, gets an order to buy a given stock. He sees that a large order could have a market-moving impact, so he purchases the stock for his own account in front of the customer. The customer's order is then filled at a higher price, in which case the specialist may or may not be the one selling to him. Depending on the size of the order, the profit to the specialist could be hundreds or many thousands of dollars.

If you want to throw up your hands in frustration, don't be concerned that there isn't a solution to the stop-loss problem. The answer has to be about the situation on the ground: how, in short, the market is behaving in terms of your overall price objective. Much of what we do in purchasing low-priced stocks is to probe the market. Buying at what we perceive to be the lows is called bottom-fishing. (In some quarters, however, the practice is characterized as trying to catch a knife.) We are trying, in a limited fashion, to find a stock at a price that will appear cheap weeks or months from now, once it rallies. There could be fundamental reasons for our decision to buy at this price, or it could be for purely technical reasons. We may have just wanted to take a flier. The risk is that the stock continues to decline—or, God forbid, it becomes totally worthless. I've had the misfortune to own four separate stocks that became totally worthless in the past 10 to 15 years. One of them actually proved to be a good moneymaker because I had the sense to see the handwriting on the wall and got out. The other three were wake-up calls. One was only for a hundred shares on an Internet stock in the bubble. But one ended up costing six figures. How can a knowledgeable and reasonable investor make such a mistake? It is actually quite easy. You let down your guard, you deny what reality is telling you, and then you compound the problem by trying to get aggressive—in short, the perfect prescription for disaster. The only answer to this type of foolishness is discipline. You must set goals in terms of both time and price. And then you must be rigorous in seeing that your benchmarks are met, or you must exit the position as soon as possible. It is the old story about the road to hell being paved with good intentions.

In placing a stop, remember what we said about a new low occurring before a run-up in a stock. Taking one last run at the stops is the oldest trick in the book. Don't be the person to sell out your position at the 52-week low! To avoid this scenario, I prefer to use what are known as mental stops—stops that are not on file with your brokerage but exist only in your head. That way, if there is a fishing expedition below the recent lows, you aren't stopped at the bottom. This requires a lot of discipline. If the move down is legitimate, you must be willing to exit the position. Should you place a stop? That depends on your ability to admit your mistakes and how closely you can watch the market. By not placing a stop, you are not saying you won't get out if the market goes against you. Rather, you are saying you are willing to get out, but you do not want to be a victim of stop-running.

We have mentioned that not all stocks trade the same. Some stocks are more volatile than other stocks. You must account for this difference in volatility in placing stops. The higher the volatility, the greater the distance away from the market price the stop should be placed. One measure of volatility is known as beta. Beta measures a stock's volatility in terms of other stocks. A high-beta stock requires a stop be placed further away than a low-beta stock. The obvious downside of a tight stop is that your position is sold on a random move and the stock subsequently soars away without you.

Stops can also be used to protect profits. Once you have profits in a position, you can use what is known as a trailing stop to follow the trend higher. The trailing stop will rise with the price level. Because it is not automatic, however, you must move the stop each time you want to change the stop. If you are using a full-service broker, you can ask your broker to trail the stop for you. Again, the downside is that a momentary drop in price will activate the stop.

Some investors use prior lows to set stops. This is fine as long as you understand that by placing your stop just below the support, you will occasionally find your position stopped out. As you can see, stop placement is an art form that often places the investor between the proverbial rock and a hard place. If you place a stop and it is hit, you may regret it; if you don't place a stop, you may also regret it. Finally, whether you use stops or not, you must remember the importance of keeping losses small. Small losses, once taken, are soon forgotten. But when you get stubborn and let a small loss grow into a large loss, the error will haunt you for years to come—not to mention the devastation it can create in your retirement account.

STOCKS THAT TREND WELL ...

Some stocks trend better than other stocks. As a rule, when I buy a stock and it completes a good trend, I sell the stock and then move on to something else. I rarely go back and trade the same stock again. But some stocks leave you with such a pleasant feeling that they become like old friends you've lost touch with. You would love to hear from them, but you just don't make the effort to pick up the phone and call. One such stock, which has given me nothing but pleasant memories, is Kulicke and Soffa Industries (KLIC), a maker of semiconductor assembly tools and a top supplier of wire bonding equipment that computer chip makers use to package circuits into finished devices. The company operates in a cyclical market that more or less tracks the fortunes of the semiconductor industry.

My love affair with Kulicke and Soffa began several years ago when I purchased 8,000 or 9,000 shares between $5 and $6 and it promptly went to the $9 to $10 area, where I sold the stock. See Figure 3.11. I remember the stock holding the trendline like a Ferrari holds the road. There were no surprises, only a steady price appreciation. Once I sold the stock, I forgot all about it. Several months ago, I was scrolling through some charts and found KLIC. The stock was back down at the $5 and $6 support level

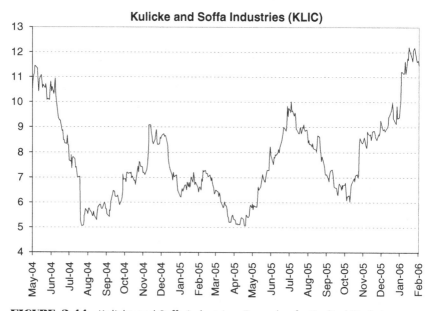

FIGURE 3.11 Kulicke and Soffa Industries: Example of a Cyclical Market

where I'd purchased it several years ago. I thought at the time this was probably a good buy, but as so often happens in the market, I was preoccupied with other stocks at the time, and I moved on without buying it. I recently glanced at the KLIC chart again. Kulicke and Soffa had made another trend-hugging rally right back up to the $9 and $10 share level. This stock was a piece of cake.

When you find a cyclical stock that tends to trend well, keep the stock on your radar screen. In the case of Kulicke and Soffa, had you been a short seller, you could have made the same money going down because it trended well in either direction. The logical place for the stock to stop declining was, of course, the prior support. And then it changed direction and went back to the prior resistance. I'm not suggesting it is a buy at its old resistance—or even a sell. But the characteristics of a stock, such as its ability to trend well, tend to persist. Clearly, with some stocks you can go back again and again . . . just as it is with old friends.

...AND THOSE THAT DON'T

In other instances, a stock's behavior is emblematic of everything a company does wrong. Several years ago, I made a major mistake in aggressively buying a start-up and unproven biotech that behaved like an indecisive teenager. This stock was all over the map as rumors flew touting its new breakthrough drugs. Particularly troubling, however, was the intransigence of management, who refused to commit themselves to saying anything to shareholders or to the press. They couldn't even commit to telling the financial community the date of an earnings report or press release. It was one frustration after another. Tossed back and forth, with a stock price bouncing all over the place, I finally threw in the towel and took a considerable loss. I never realized that I could dislike a company or a stock with such intensity.

Then one day the phone rang.

"Did you see the news on ABCD?" my friend asked, using the symbol for the biotech.

"ABCD," I said. "Don't ever mention that stock to me again."

"Well something is driving it higher," she said. "It's up over 100 percent in two days."

"Don't mention that stock to me ever again," I repeated.

"Well, I'm going to buy it," she insisted.

"Buy it? You mean sell."

"I'm buying it right now," she said.

"Go ahead," I said. "Buy the top."

And she did. After that, the stock broke hard and began behaving like . . . well, a teenager with a multiple personality disorder. I later learned that she had sold it at a loss. I don't regret leaving that stock alone.

Looking back, I remember how the stock's potentially explosive behavior was something that I misperceived to mean it was ready to run. The stock's price gyrations were nothing more than the Street's reactions to the hype. Whenever you see the words *breakthrough, explosive growth, untapped potential,* watch out! This was a company with no earnings and a history of failed drug tests. Even the chart looked like the stock was giving you the finger. The promise couldn't match the reality. The stock price ultimately reflected that failed promise. It went down.

We are talking about polar extremes here: the ideal trending stock against the overhyped and potentially fraudulent highflier. In the thousands of listed stocks trading on the major exchanges, there are ample supplies of both.

THE REBOUND THEORY

Connoisseurs of racetrack handicapping will tell you that thoroughbreds that perform poorly in two or three races often bounce back to front-running form. Good horses, goes the theory, are just too talented to allow a blocked trip or poor start out of the gate to hold them back. Another theory is that the trainers of proven winners may even use some races as preparation for a high-stakes race in the future. In other words, they aren't really trying to win!

In the world of stocks, you might translate this theory to mean that a good company that temporarily falls out of favor with investors will rebound back to its prior heights, or conversely, a company that gets ahead of itself in the valuation game might fall back to more realistic levels.

My experience with Kulicke and Soffa Industries certainly demonstrated this fact. When it fell back to its prior support, I was frankly surprised. I thought the stock would find a support at a higher level. But given time, Kulicke and Soffa, like so many other stocks, went back to its prior highs, a climb that you can readily see is necessary if it is ever going to break out and trend even higher. What it is about some stocks that keep rebounding back to former resistance levels?

One school of thought that has gained popularity in the academic community over the years is that security prices are purely random. Perhaps. But I can tell you from experience that the professional investors who grow rich from the markets are anything but random. The same people reap the lion's share of the profits year after year. Like any competitive enterprise, the cream rises. This so called random walk thesis may suggest that stock prices move by chance, but there is clear evidence that market winners utilize trading techniques that are anything but random.

Another school of thought, however, is less inclined to accept the random walk theory. These financial researchers are increasingly supporting the notion that stock market patterns can be analyzed and successfully traded. The technical analyst crowd is increasingly gaining respectability by demonstrating that price patterns do have a rhyme and reason. The bottom line: Perhaps future prices can be predicted by past performance.

I would like to see a study that quantifies the potential of a stock rising after three strong attempts to break a support level. Turning the question on its head, what if a stock challenges a resistance three times and fails to penetrate on the third attempt. Will it turn lower?

The notion of the rebound is intriguing because there is so much anecdotal evidence that sellers can have a field day with a stock until it hits a major support. At that point, no matter how much they sell, every offer will be met with a stronger bid, and the shares will ultimately rise.

One theory is that the market tends to overreact to news, both good and bad. According to this theory, a positive earnings report could potentially send a stock soaring, and set up an excellent selling situation; the other side of the coin is that bad earnings will cause a stock's price to tank, setting up a bounce scenario. Does this suggest you should buy every break and sell every rally? Well, not exactly. Some breaks and rallies are clearly meant to be faded. But if you have a breakout in a stock, it may indeed be headed higher—at least until the inevitable profit-taking phase kicks in.

While it is fun to kick around market ideas, what are the inferences to be drawn from the rebound theory? One is that beaten-down stocks are more likely to bounce. You mean Kulicke and Soffa is a better buy at $6 a share than it is at $10? Apparently. Additional evidence suggests that weaker stocks over a fixed time period are likely to do better in the future than stronger stocks over the same period of time. Put another way, the stronger issues have already made their move; the weaker ones haven't.

Take a troubled company like Krispy Kreme Doughnuts (KKD). This once highflier lost more than 78 percent of its value in recent months. Over the past year, it traded in a range of $13 a share and $2.50 a share, in round numbers. The current price is $3. A quick glance at the chart shows that it has challenged the support at $3 on two separate occasions. One would think, without knowing the fundamentals, that KKD is worth a cautious buy between $5 and $3 a share. The bad news is already out, and any additional negative news would probably be discounted. See Figure 3.12.

Borrowing on our horse-racing analogy, consider this: When an odds-on front-runner, who is expected to win, holds back and claims only show money, his image is somewhat tarnished because he was expected to win

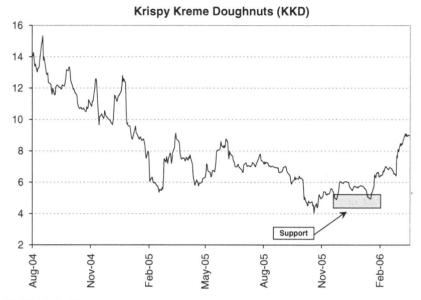

FIGURE 3.12 Krispy Kreme Shows Signs of Support at $3 per Share

the race. The next time he runs, his odds are likely to be longer because bettors no longer have confidence in his abilities. Higher odds means a better payoff, of course, to his backers if he wins. In the stock market, studies clearly demonstrate that beaten-down stocks (unlikely winners) register impressive gains when and if they are discovered and make it to the finish line!

There is little doubt that you will be able to locate dozens of candidates among low-priced stocks that could be tomorrow's big winner. Even a casual glance at several stock charts reveals potential bounce candidates:

- Propelled by the oil boom, Grey Wolf, Inc. (GW), the owner of drilling rigs, soared from under $3 to over $8 on the bullish news of high oil prices. See Figure 3.13.
- Hong Kong–based Euro Tech Holdings (CLWT) has formed a strong base at $3. This is a saucer pattern on the chart signaling higher prices ahead. See Figure 3.14.
- Escalon Medical Corp. (ESMC), a medical stock, was beaten down in price from over $13 to under $3 a share in recent months. See Figure 3.15.
- Genaera Corporation (GENR) is a biopharmaceutical company that has been beaten down from a 52-week high of $4.35 a share to its 52-week low of $1.32 a share. See Figure 3.16.

FIGURE 3.13 Grey Wolf, Inc., Soars as a Result of Bullish News

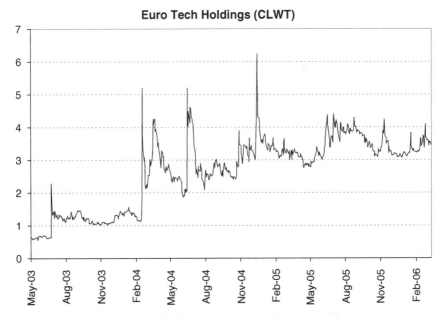

FIGURE 3.14 Euro Tech Holdings Signals Higher Prices Ahead

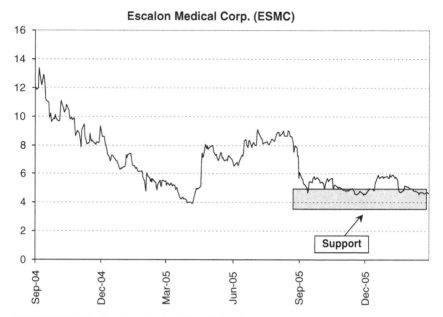

FIGURE 3.15 Escalon Medical Corp.'s Decline

FIGURE 3.16 Genaera Corporation at Its 52-Week Low

- Knology, Inc. (KNOL) is a provider of wireless services in nine markets in the southeastern United States. The stock had formed a strong support prior to its current rally, which later extended to almost $20 a share. See Figure 3.17.

TIMING THE REBOUND

Investors are an impatient lot. I know because I used to be a day trader in the futures market. My time horizon was rarely over 30 minutes. But when you position long-term stock purchases, you are trying to participate in the growth of a maturing company, and that takes time. While it is an ideal practice to try to pinpoint the exact bottoming of a stock, it is notoriously difficult. You may be early, or you may be late. As long as you can ultimately buy near the bottom, however, it doesn't make a big difference.

Back in the introduction, I stressed that every company has its story. You will find that a company's biography is a fluid story, one that changes from month to month and year to year, just as you are one person in your twenties and yet another in your forties and still another in your sixties. You grow and change, and companies do as well. I am reminded of the Mark Twain line about a young man who said, "When I was sixteen I couldn't believe what a jerk my father was. But by the time I turned twenty

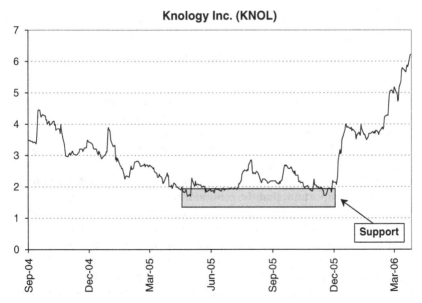

FIGURE 3.17 Knology, Inc., Rallies

I couldn't believe how much the old man had learned in four years." With companies, the aging process often takes place beyond the vision of the investor. Business plans that are put into practice today may not yield results for several years. For this reason, you have to choose a company with a corporate vision that will yield results in the years to come.

When a company is out of favor, the best opportunities exist. That's the time to focus on finding the best deal, the cheap stock. When you buy a stock for $1 a share and you are later able to sell the same stock for $10 a share, it is a truly remarkable occurrence. The stock has acquired value during the period you owned it. For new buyers, $10 a share is probably reasonable. But looking back, you cannot believe you once paid just $1 for the same share of stock.

How do you find such bargains? Well, first you have to open up your thinking to the realm of what is possible. No one knows the future, but new technology and new inventions open up possibilities that we never knew existed. Given the right management, companies can transform themselves. They can get out of unprofitable enterprises and into profitable ones. They can merge with other companies or issue IPOs to raise cash to finance current operations. There are myriad opportunities available.

Almost all of these operations take time. It cannot be done overnight. As a result, the investor must be patient and allow management time to put its plan into place. Ideally, you have researched the company whose shares you wish to purchase. But there are many things that can go wrong. Not only must you select the right stock to buy, you must also select the right time to purchase it. You have both stock risk and market risk. Even the best stock is hammered down in a bad market. So if your stock isn't performing, perhaps you need to look at the market. We recently had a market that was characterized by months and months of declining prices. Because I was already long stock, I had undoubtedly purchased too early. By waiting, I could have saved myself a lot of money. But of course, I didn't know that at the time. By glancing at dozens of price charts, I realized I wasn't alone. The entire market was declining.

Finally, without announcing itself, the market bottomed one day, and now, several months later, those of us who held through the decline are starting to see impressive gains. I earnestly suspect the bottom is behind us and, more important, that the rebound, still in its infancy, has just begun. Given today's chart patterns, look for better days ahead.

To fully realize the potential gains of a rebound situation, you probably want to wait from 18 months to 30 months. Most investors want a sure-thing. That's why they are never going to be around in the early stages of a significant price rise. Stocks don't start to gain attention until they are already high. That's why everyone wants to own Disney or Wal-Mart or Microsoft: Their stories are already household names. Significantly, the real growth spurts occur between the second and third year following a stock turnaround. In order to participate in this growth, you clearly need to be in the right place at the right time, and that requires buying early.

Stocks don't announce their intentions to trade higher—but they often do. For that matter, analysts and other market pundits, who are notoriously late in broadcasting a stock's arrival, rarely see its ascendancy before it is under way. The idea is to find a low-priced stock before it gets on anyone else's radar screen. One place to look is the stocks making the new lows column in your local newspaper. Granted, some of these issues are mortally wounded and won't be coming back. But others are simply experiencing temporary setbacks. Charts don't lie when it comes to tracking a stock. If you find a stock that has declined to its lows and is now trending sideways, it may be setting up a base. It is from this base that shares ultimately trade higher. Look for support that holds or support that has been violated, followed by a recovery back above the support line. You also want to look for ascending triangles and other bullish chart patterns that point to higher prices ahead.

Do not expect immediate results. Out-of-favor stocks often take months to regain their luster. Once you have experience in reading chart patterns, you will notice that some stocks become tightly coiled as the ultimate breakout day approaches. This is a sign that you should be loading the boat. Once the breakout occurs, the stock won't trade at those bargain-basement prices ever again.

Many stocks fall into this category. They will be beaten down, only to trade sideways for a time. Only then do they rise. This first bullish leg is then followed by a period of declining-to-sideways trading, presenting another buying opportunity at a higher level. At that point, the stage is set for a resumption of the trend higher as the second leg is formed. This is the classic out-of-favor stock staging a recovery.

The chart for TIBCO Software, Inc. (TIBX) is a perfect example of a newly unpopular stock among investors. See Figure 3.18. The recent annual range was roughly $5.50 at the low to $13.50 at the high. After an impressive rally, the stock fell out of favor and retraced most of its move back to the lows. At that stage, a sideways consolidation began, signaling yet another opportunity to buy the stock prior to a run to the previous 52-week highs. How do we know the stock won't fall out the bottom of the support? We don't. But the odds don't favor that scenario when the support has held for so long. None of the buyers in the $6 and $7 support area have experienced much, if any, adversity. Meanwhile, the sellers of the stock have seen their selling activities met with strong buying. As to where the top might be, simply look at the well-formed prior leg in the rally. The stock has already demonstrated its ability to rally. It recently traded above $8 a share.

If you look back several years further, you will find that Time Warner Telecom, Inc. (TWTC) was a dirt-cheap stock selling under $1 a share. See Figure 3.19. Now this was an opportunity. Within two years, it soared above

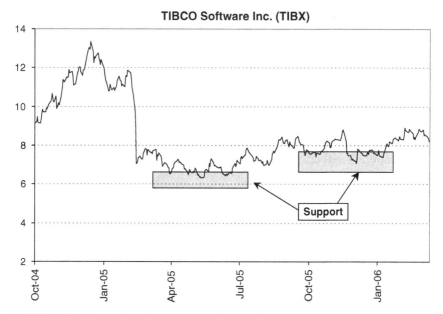

FIGURE 3.18   TIBCO Software Inc. Falls Out of Favor with Investors

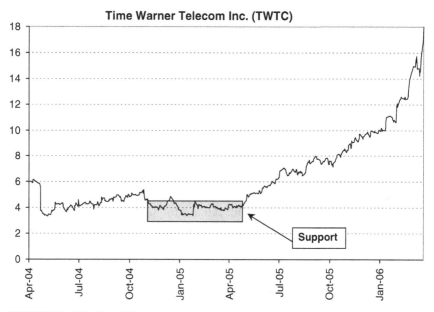

FIGURE 3.19   Time Warner Telecom, Inc.: Opportunity

$12 a share. At this point, the stock was ready to retrace—and it did. Prices subsequently traded down to $4 a share, where it predictably formed a strong consolidation pattern in the $5 a share area. Since then, it has begun its inevitable climb back to form the second leg. It is now trading above $20 a share.

A stock that until recently was on the ropes but is now attracting wide investor participation is JDS Uniphase Corporation (JDSU), the fiber-optics company. See Figure 3.20. In the past two years, the stock has disappointed investors again and again, but the chart tells a different story. Having based and formed strong support, the precise pattern that encourages investors to pick up shares, the stock has soared higher.

There are many, many examples of stocks that have never made their run, ran and collapsed, or have simply been ignored by the investment community.

The Kansas City–based Aquila, Inc. (ILA) is a company with which I am very familiar because I used to own it at approximately 10 times its current

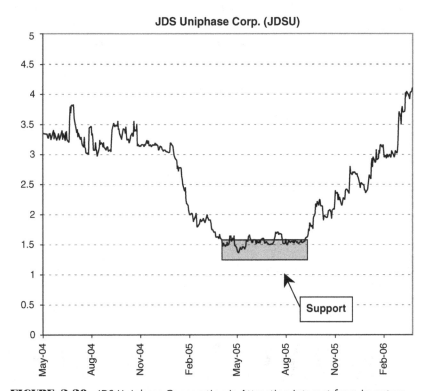

FIGURE 3.20 JDS Uniphase Corporation Is Attracting Interest from Investors

value. I was fortunate and sold the company long before it began its slide from over $35 a share to under $5 a share. Currently, trading near $3.50, this electric and natural gas utility has a 52-week range between $4.24 and $2.90. At these levels, the stock shows promise to move higher, even if it is unlikely to ever again reach its lofty heights. See Figure 3.21.

Zhone Technologies, Inc. (ZHNE), which builds communications and network equipment for phone companies and cable operators, is a classic example of a beaten-down stock. Several years ago, the stock traded as high as $6 a share. But then the shares plummeted to under $2. Over the past year, the company has traded between $1.06 and $1.64. Shares currently are trading hands at approximately $1.20 a share. See Figure 3.22.

Although none of these companies may offer buying opportunities at the time you read this material, they all illustrate the potential of stocks that are ready to bounce or have already bounced. Be assured that many, many other stocks offer similar potential. Research in Motion, Inc. (RIMM), the Canadian-based company that markets the popular BlackBerry wireless device, is another classic standout of the beaten-down security. At one point selling for approximately $50 a share, the company's stock plummeted below $10, where it languished for months before skyrocketing to a presplit price of over $100 a share. Today, the stock trades above $100 a share, but it was once dirt-cheap, under $10. See Figure 3.23.

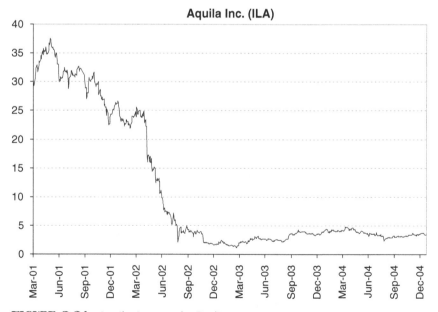

FIGURE 3.21   Aquila, Inc., on the Decline

FIGURE 3.22 Zhone Technologies, Inc.: Classic Beaten-Down Stock

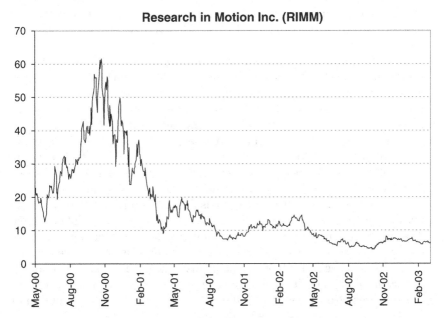

FIGURE 3.23 RIMM: Another Classic Beaten-Down Security

WHEN IS A STOCK READY TO BUY?

The short answer is simple: when it is ready to go up. The longer answer requires more explanation. To begin our discussion, let's concentrate on the buy side of the equation as opposed to short selling. There's a place for short selling in the market, but when you are concentrating on low-priced shares, as we are here, you are better off sticking with the long side of the market.

As you can see from our discussion thus far, share prices, for a variety of reasons, frequently lose favor and are beaten down. Just as the 80-to-1 shot in a maiden race doesn't understand the long odds against it, companies, with few exceptions, don't undertake their day-to-day operations with an eye on the share price. Apart from suddenly producing surprisingly results, there is little a company can do to promote higher share prices other than to run their best race. As a result, companies frequently get what is called technically oversold. This means that the bias in the market, for a multitude of reasons, is to undervalue the company's shares.

We don't need to go into the many reasons why a company might be technically oversold. Bad earnings, a bear market, management shenanigans, an incompetent conference call presentation, lawsuits—the reasons go on and on. The point is that the company's shares are taking a beating, and there is an underlying golden opportunity for astute investors to take advantage of the situation. I know what you are thinking: Okay, tell me how!

The first step is to develop a built-in radar screen for technical breakdowns in the market. Has a long-standing trendline been broken? The price action will trigger stops. Share prices should start to decline and trend lower. Bearish sentiment builds. At this stage, the mounting hopelessness of the situation is sowing the seeds of the next bull market in the stock. But there are few observers of this fact because the sellers are busy jumping ship. In the rush to the exits, the downward momentum builds. In due time—it could be weeks, it could be months—the last seller sells. At this point, you must remember that market breaks are never accomplished in a vacuum. For every share sold, there is a share purchased. It may not occur in a one-to-one fashion, however. A hundred sellers may sell in a panic to a single well-financed buyer. The number of shareholders may have decreased, but the number of shares most assuredly has not. I have a friend who routinely begins his buying campaigns by acquiring a couple of million shares in a company. Do you think he finds three or four sellers to sell him those shares? No. He buys 10,000 here, 5,000 there, and over a period of weeks or months, he acquires his position.

At the bottom, a stock may have been languishing. But more often than not, the bottom is formed in a series of panicked, distressed selling campaigns, punctuated by an occasion price spike. This kind of price action is not easy on the nerves for either buyer or seller. The bear juggernaut does not give up the ghost readily. Even temporary rallies are initially met by massive selling. But in the end, the support will hold and the stock will rise. When the downturn is fully put to rest, the technical indicators immediately become positive. This is the sign that the trend has changed. The fundamentals will be next to fall into line.

Consider the situation in Sun Microsystems, Inc. (JAVA), once a darling of the Street that has fallen out of favor in recent years. The stock has made a round-trip from $3.50 to $5.50 in recent years. In completing its pattern, the stock's chart finished the inverted-V pattern. It is now trading near $19 a share. See Figure 3.24.

Was the stock oversold at $3.50 a share after topping at $5.50? You bet. A number of technical indicators, most of which we haven't covered yet, pointed toward an oversold condition. The problem is that no one wants to catch a falling knife. It will take time for Sun's shares to regain the enthusiastic support of the investor community.

Some stocks culminate their bear markets in what are known as selling climaxes. JDS Uniphase, mentioned earlier, had such a one-day selling climax when it fell to its 52-week low at $1.32 a share. The stock closed near the higher end of its range on the day, a sign that the downward move was over. It then traded higher to over $1.75 a share and is currently trading

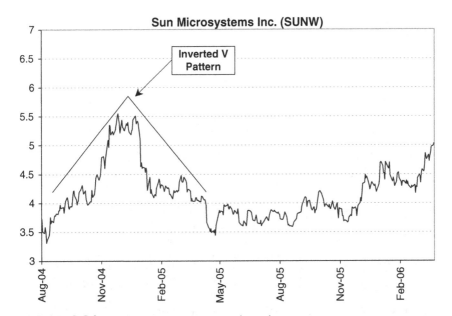

FIGURE 3.24 Sun Microsystems, Inc., Rebounds

at $4.11. The selling climax marked the end of a prolonged and persistent decline that extended all the way down from over $5.

Can we say that the selling climax pinpointed the end of the bear market in JDSU shares? Although nothing is ever certain, probably the long nightmare is finally over for the company's shareholders. The stock has been enjoying exceptional volume in recent weeks.

Even a casual glance at a Lucent Technologies, Inc. (LU) chart demonstrates how clearly the downward trendline was broken in recent months as that troubled company began to trend higher. See Figure 3.25. When you have a company like Lucent, you have a lot of unhappy investors. Just a few years ago, the company traded above $80 a share prior to its plunge to the bottom, where it found support in the $1 to $2 range. Any rally in a stock like this is apt to bring out sellers who would rather have something than nothing. Nevertheless, the company's shares have a bullish bias these days, now that the final selling climax has finally occurred.

A basic tenet of technical analysis is that you let the stock's price action do the talking. Technicians are quick to ignore fundamental factors because they believe the stock's entire story is tied up in one simple statistic: the market price. That price is where both buyers and sellers have come into agreement about a particular stock's intrinsic value. The buyers are willing to purchase at that price, and the sellers are willing to sell at that price.

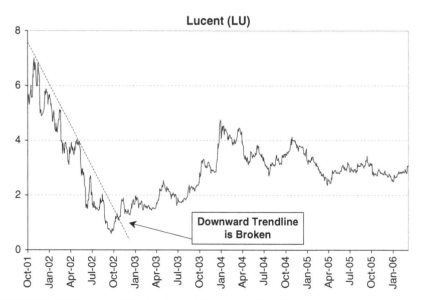

FIGURE 3.25 Lucent Technologies' Downward Trend

Now that you have an established equilibrium price, where both buyers and sellers are in agreement, you need a counterforce to enter into the market to move the price either higher or lower. There are no shortages of factors that could provide this counterforce. You might have an analyst put out a buy recommendation on the stock, or the company CEO might appear on CNBC. The Fed could lower rates, and the stock market as a whole might enjoy several days of higher prices. There's a saying in financial circles that the market is always right. That means, regardless of your expectations, dreams, and hopes, you must ultimately respect the valuation that the market places on a stock. While Street pundits can easily talk up a stock's prospects, the market knows better. A vivid illustration of this concept occurred in the final days of Enron, when Kenneth Lay, the company CEO, tried to assure his employees, many of whom had their life savings in the company stock, that the prospects for the company's future were great and that he, the chairman, was actually purchasing shares. This, of course, was a lie. Lay had been selling his shares. It didn't take the market long to see through this falsehood. The shares plummeted and finally stabilized at their true value, zero.

Remember, as a would-be technician, you want to let the stock's technical status tell you where the shares are headed. In looking at a chart pattern, ask: Where is this stock going? Stocks that bottom are often forming a base, which can be a highly bullish sign. A stock can be down and not out. Or a stock can be down and hopeless. The two are quite different. Let the crowd purchase the glamour stocks. The real profits are to be made among those shares that are down and not out.

Speaking of glamour stocks, take a quick look at Microsoft Corporation (MSFT) share prices. Over the past year, Microsoft has traded roughly between $37 and $26 a share (see Figure 3.26). Most of that time, the stock has been trending lower. The stock is currently trading around $35. This is a stock that everyone wants to own. But the question is why?

Contrast that price action with the past year's trading activity in a little-known San Diego–based biotech known as Illumina, Inc. (ILMN). Illumina has made two classic legs higher off its $4 lows. The first leg extended from $4 to $10.50 a share. Following a very predictable pullback and consolidation, the stock gathered support at $7 a share and doubled in price to over $16 a share. Illumina is currently trading at $56. See Figure 3.27.

This is the precise type of price action that I think about when I hear you cannot make money trading low-priced stocks: a stock trading at $4 that goes to $27. What's more, if you went back two years, you could have picked up Illumina shares for $2. So you would have already had a 100 percent gain before the more recent buyers showed up at $4 a share. Was this a beaten-down stock? You bet. Down—but clearly not out! The Microsoft buyer, on the other hand, would have had to be content with dividends.

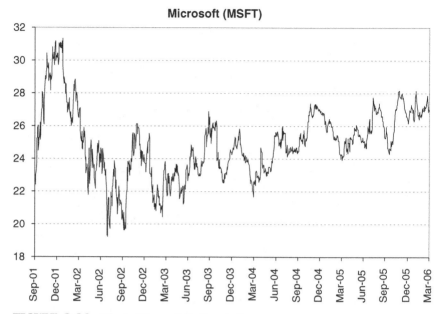

FIGURE 3.26 Why Is Microsoft So Popular?

FIGURE 3.27 Illumina: A Much Better Choice

Going back three years, Microsoft has remained a $20+ stock. Today, it is still trading just above $28 a share.

Never underestimate the potential for a bounce in a beaten-down stock. The Santa Clara, California–based Internet software provider Extreme Networks, Inc. (EXTR) provides an excellent example of a stock that has climbed the mountain, only to totally descend on the other side. In a technical sense, this stock is poised for a rebound. See Figure 3.28.

The same could be said for the London-based Danka Business Systems (ADR) (DANKY), which has tanked from $4 to $1.25 over the past year. The stock later rallied to $2.80 a share. It subsequently sold off from there. See Figure 3.29. There is a thinking in the market that a stock that has already traded at one price is likely to trade there again, as opposed to a stock that has never risen off its initial IPO low-price origins.

We've mentioned that it is important to track volume when a stock is breaking out and getting ready to run. But there are subtle clues given by the volume statistics that also tell you when a countermove is imminent. Volume is an important tool of technical analysis because it can provide a glimpse of the quality of the buying and selling. In general, volume follows the trend. But when the minor trend (as in a pullback scenario) is against the major trend (up), the drying up of the volume tells you the minor trend is over. For example, the stock makes a powerful move higher, and the

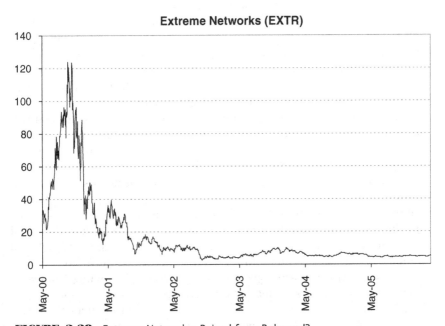

Extreme Networks (EXTR)

FIGURE 3.28 Extreme Networks: Poised for a Rebound?

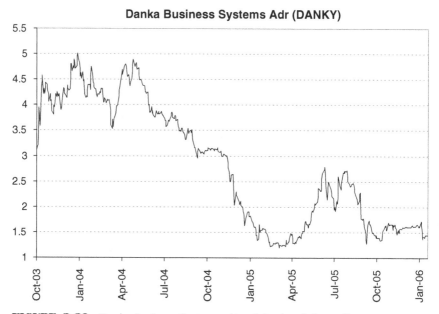

FIGURE 3.29   Danka Business Systems: Also Poised to Rebound?

inevitable pullback begins. Where do you buy the stock? When the downward move is essentially halted and the volume dries up. Let's say your stock trades a million shares a day on average. If you get a 400,000 volume day and prices are just drifting in a narrow range, chances are the stock is ready to resume its upward path. The same, of course, applies to the major trend once you have had a significant move higher. The volume dries up at the top, signaling the beginning of the countertrend lower.

Take some time and begin to monitor your stock's volume. You will undoubtedly find that, while volume expands on the breakout day, the real thrust in higher volume occurs the day after the breakout. This should come as no surprise. With most investors waiting for a stock to demonstrate some promise prior to risking their investment dollars, the surge in volume occurs a day later. On the second day up, however, the stock is vulnerable to profit-taking. And by the third day up, the technical situation becomes downright hazardous. For this reason, if you miss the initial breakout, you are often better off waiting for the inevitable pullback and jumping aboard as a buyer on lower volume on the countertrend.

To summarize: Overbought markets experience declining volume as they near a top; oversold markets experience declining volume as they near a bottom. In either case, the quality of the volume signals the reversal. The stock typically rises on increasing volume only after the primary trend is once again intact. It is important to understand the context of the volume—not just whether the market is momentarily rising or falling.

The other place to pay close attention to volume is at major bottoms. We've discussed that when the last seller sells, the stock is often severely oversold, and the trend is likely to reverse and bounce higher. This reversal is often accomplished on dull volume following the high-volume trading sessions when the stock is in a free fall. A stock, seeking a bottom, often falls on dull volume and immediately bounces higher. This is especially bullish when the closing price is at the higher end of the day's range because that is the classic key reversal day pattern. In this instance, the volume confirms the price action in a technical sense. The selling is now done. The time has come to be an aggressive buyer because the odds now favor the long side of the market.

One word of warning, however, is due. What appears to be the major bottom may not be. Given the sheer perversity of the market, prices may be due for another trip under the lows. At that point, the bottom-fishers may indeed panic and send the market lower yet. But this, again, is a time for opportunity. You can often buy this break on a market order. If the purchase is immediately profitable, you will know you now have a technically strong market. Understandably, just about everyone is reluctant to jump into a stock that is in the process of making new lows. This is why almost no one actually buys at the low of a move.

HOW TO IDENTIFY THE LOW-RISK BUY

Risk-conscious investors make every effort to place their buy orders near valid support levels. From the previous discussion, you can see that not all buying campaigns are equal in risk. Trying to pick a bottom, for example, near 52-week lows can be a hazardous operation, even if the stock is technically oversold. Who's to say that particular stock won't become even more oversold? Users of the much-loved stochastics oscillators, which measure relative strength, are quick to tell you that an indicator can signal technical weakness long before the turn in the market. For this reason, intelligent investors are constantly looking to refine their skills in terms of selecting low-risk buying opportunities.

Perhaps the safest place to buy a stock is on a countermove off a major upswing. By that time, the stock has already demonstrated its intention of wanting to get somewhere in a hurry. The countermove is just the way the stock catches its breath following a rigorous race higher. For this reason, technicians are forever calculating retracement levels when a stock powers higher.

The best-known of these retracement levels is, of course, the Fibonacci 0.618 retracement. Fibonacci was a medieval mathematician who tried to discover truths about the universe that seemed to adhere to mathematical formulas. Handed down through the centuries, the power of 0.618 seems to be his most enduring contribution.

As a practical matter, there are two things you need to know about using this simple formula. One, buy and sell stops tend to be clustered around this point. Two, the countermove in the market may approach the 0.618 level but may not actually reach it. The implications of these two statements are as follows: First, you want to be careful about using a stop near the 0.618; second, you may want to be a buyer well before the 0.618 is approached.

When looking to buy a stock by utilizing the Fibonacci retrace point, you simply calculate the magnitude of the range prior to the pullback and multiply by 0.618. Then take the resultant number and subtract it from the high of the move.

For example, a stock trends higher, rising from $7 to $10. The trend is, therefore, $3 in length. As the market begins its countermove lower, multiply the $3 move by 0.618. The answer is $1.85 when rounded. You then subtract this number from the high of the move—in this case, $10. The 0.618 retrace number is $8.15 ($10.00 − $1.85 = $8.15).

As prices approach this number, they should find support. This trade is considered relatively safe because you can place a sell stop just below the retrace number, thereby limiting your risk. The upside potential, of course, far exceeds the downside risk of loss.

This, in a nutshell, is the theory. You can measure 0.618 numbers in declining markets as well. In a declining market, of course, the 0.618 pinpoints the resistance of the move higher as opposed to the support on a move lower when you are buying.

Now let's turn to a handful of stocks that have made recent rallies to see where the countermove stabilized prior to moving higher:

- Agilent Technologies, Inc. (A) recently trended from $21 to $25 a share. The 0.618 retrace number was approximately $22.50. The countermove stopped at $23 before rising $10 higher, above $33.50. The stock is currently near $35 a share. See Figure 3.30.
- Motorola, Inc. (MOT) went from approximately $8 to $20 prior to the countermove that stabilized above $14. Then it rose back to $24. The 0.618 retrace price was near $12.50. See Figure 3.31.
- Colgate-Palmolive Company (CL) trended up $11 from $44 a share to $55 a share. The 0.618 was approximately $48.20. The countermove down found support just below $49 a share. See Figure 3.32.

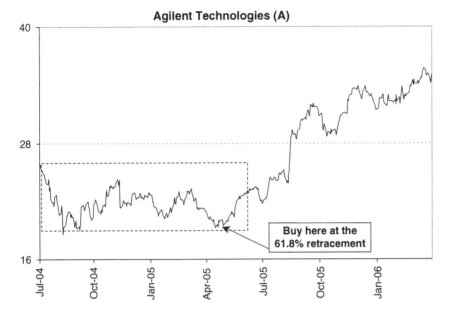

FIGURE 3.30 Agilent Technologies

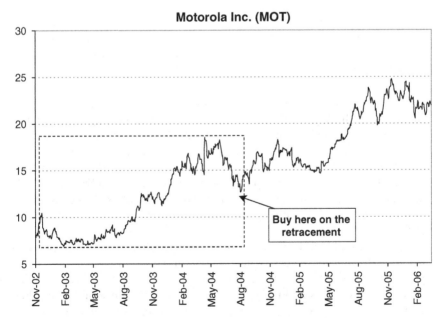

FIGURE 3.31 Motorola, Inc.

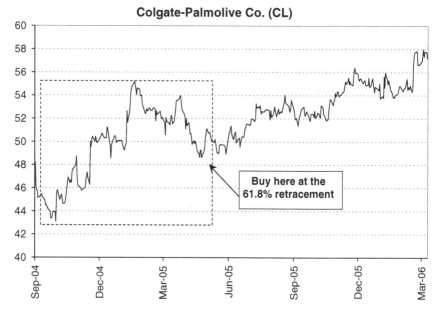

FIGURE 3.32 Colgate Palmolive Company

- Siemens AG (SI) rose from just under $66 a share to $85 a share. The 0.618 retrace price was approximately $73.25—and that's where the countermove down stopped. The stock doubled from there. See Figure 3.33.

In each of these cases, the countermove stabilized at or slightly above the 0.618. At those price levels, you had a low-risk buying opportunity. For many investors, buying on breaks is counterintuitive. They don't want to be buying when sellers are driving the market lower. But this is precisely where low-risk buying can be accomplished: at or near the 0.618 retrace price. I have used this entry point for many years in my LSS 3-day Cycle Method trading system and in my time and price studies. The results suggest that one of the safest places to buy is after a rally on the countermove pullback.

The principle holds whether you are day trading or long-term position trading. The market tends to trade in wave and counterwave cycles. When you place a low-risk buy on a countermove, you don't have to risk buying a failed breakout. Nor do you have to worry about chasing the market, another hazardous strategy. Rather, you let the market come to you and stabilize with a close stop always in mind. The key is finding a bullish chart in the first instance. The downside is that you must be patient in selecting

FIGURE 3.33 Siemens

the trade and that a truly strong market may not retrace sufficiently for you to enter the position at all.

The idea is not to panic when an unanticipated event occurs in the market but rather to try to understand the phenomenon driving the price action. You can be sure that investors who sell the bottom are thinking about one thing—the money. This is a mistake. The correct approach is to analyze the situation and, when appropriate, take action. Whenever prices advance higher, there is a safety zone below the market into which prices can retreat, providing a breather prior to reasserting their trajectory higher. As mentioned previously, this is clearly and easily defined by the 0.618 retrace pattern. There is no guarantee that prices will reach the 0.618 retrace price or, for that matter, that if they do, they won't trade lower. But the probabilities favor a cooling-off period immediately following a strong run, and that's exactly what often happens. When you understand a given market phenomenon, it's a lot easier to keep your wits about you while everyone else is losing theirs. Learn to identify low-risk buying opportunities, and your bottom line will show robust profits. You do this by thinking about the market, not the money.

I know what you are thinking here: How do you know to buy more? What if the stock had continued to fall? The one-word answer is experience. On the initial panic selling, the stock may have behaved as it always does on a less-than-stellar earnings report. Let's say it broke hard to the support level. This means that all the hapless buyers who purchased in anticipation of higher prices lost money; they were massacring themselves in a wholesale run to the exits. I had a feeling of déjà vu; if I'd seen this once, I'd seen it more than 100 times. So when you find yourself with an abundance of lemons, the situation calls for making lemonade. The best opportunities are often unexpected. You'd be surprised how often not getting what you want in the market, as in life, turns out to be a blessing in disguise.

The rule is that stocks spend a lot of time at support and resistance levels, trading within the consolidation zone. They then make sudden price moves to new support levels, where they stabilize in price prior to surging higher.

Describing how a stock signals it is a low-risk buying opportunity can become somewhat tedious. "I know an opportunity when I see one" can be less than helpful. But it certainly helps to know your stock in all its permutations. The correct approach is to let the stock's price action tell the story. The incorrect approach is to try to second-guess the stock's behavior. I have a friend who is a very reliable contrary indicator. If she is buying, I want to be selling, and vice versa. One of her passions is to take small profits when big profits are on the horizon. Just this past week, she called me and told me of selling a profitable oil stock on a modest up move. The stock has been surging higher ever since.

Taking small profits when big profits are available is one of those unforgivable sins. You need the big profits to offset the inevitable setbacks. Not long ago, I ran into a friend to whom I had recommended a stock several years ago. I'd long since taken profits in the stock and moved on, entirely forgetting my recommendation to him. He was all excited when I saw him.

"Remember that stock you told me about several years ago?"

"Yes."

"Well, I made eight times my investment," he said. "What a bonanza!"

As I said, we'd both forgotten all about the stock. I'd long since sold it at a profit, and he'd been busy with his law practice. In the meantime, the stock had had an opportunity to grow. Rather than micromanage the stock's progress, he'd simply purchased the stock and let it sit in his securities account. Sometimes, however, success such as this comes with its own drawbacks. He now thinks he can make eight times his investment on all his stocks. I explained that this kind of stock price appreciation occurs only once in a lifetime. If I'd known what was in store for the stock's price, I would have held onto the shares myself.

There are countless ways to look back on opportunities that have gotten away, but the best advice is simply to move on. In due course, other opportunities will present themselves. Just remember that every situation has its very own set of circumstances and risks. The theorists who claim that there is an ironclad guarantee with every trade are simply wrong. You must know two things to win consistent profits in the market: when to buy and when to sell. Everything else is superfluous.

In my day-trading days, I used to give weekend seminars on how to identify profitable strategies. After painstakingly outlining a complex strategy to pinpoint profitable entry points to a seminar class one weekend, an attendee raised his hand and asked if it was a good idea to initiate a short-selling position when one took profits on the initial long position. While the question was asked in good faith, I could only think of how naive it really was. Here we were spending hours trying to find two good entry spots a day to buy a market about to rally, and the questioner wanted to capture the market's turn both coming and going. It is hard enough to get on the right side going up; trying to pinpoint the breaks is even more difficult, if not impossible.

If you are ever going to truly capture the brass ring in your investment activities, you have to acquaint yourself with the nuts and bolts of your particular stock. What's the 52-week range? Where's the support? What did past price rallies look like? And if the stock is currently trading near or at a long-term support, what has held it back for so long—and why purchase the shares now? These are all legitimate and necessary questions. Has there been a sea change in this particular stock? What is the untold story that will soon be known to investors? And why do you understand the stock's potential while the Street hasn't got a clue?

Technicians spend their days trying to discern hidden bullish patterns from price charts. Fundamentalists, while trying to do the same thing, take an entirely different approach by analyzing revenues and earnings and cost factors.

I put a lot of faith in both approaches, but I'm primarily a technical analyst because I know that fundamental factors will ultimately be reflected in a stock's price. You cannot hide the fact that a stock refuses to retreat in price when sellers repeatedly try to knock the price lower. The offers, in this case, are met with strong bids, and the stock holds the support level or moves higher. In either case, it is a sign that *someone* thinks the stock is worth buying regardless of the reason and, quite frequently, in spite of continuous bearish sentiment. A stock that cannot retreat in the face of bearish news is a prime candidate for higher prices.

Don't believe me? Take a look at a chart for WCA Waste Corporation (WCAA). Here's a company in the hot environmental services field that formed a perfect inverted-V pattern on the charts, rising from $8 to $10.50 and back again. Going back two years, there is strong support for the stock at $6. Indeed, the last time it hit $6, it formed a triple bottom, one of the strongest patterns you can find. It is now trading at $6 again.

If I went back and studied the fundamentals of this stock, I bet I could find plenty of evidence why the stock traded back down to $6. But the important fact is that it held that price despite the bearish sentiment and is today trading higher. When news headlines scream about environmental problems, such as the pumping out of the flooded city of New Orleans, it only stands to reason that environmental service companies will be in strong demand in the months ahead.

WCA Waste is a small, off-the-radar company with low volume that is given to occasional volume spikes. Take a look at a chart on this stock, and you will immediately notice how the volume spikes when there is a major change in direction (Figure 3.34). Likewise, a long-standing down trendline was broken when the stock rallied off its long-term support. This is the kind of stock Wall Street rarely pays much attention to. This also means that investors will be slow to recognize its potential. Given time, however, this small environmental services company could become a regular feature in the financial press. At that point, of course, you will want to be selling your shares to some Johnny-come-lately hedge fund.

In analyzing a stock such as this one, you want to go back at least two or three years and identify the support levels. At that point, if the stock is in a downtrend, you want to identify where it should find support. At or near

FIGURE 3.34   WCA Waste Shows Volume Spikes When There Is a Major Change in Direction

that support level, you should buy the stock. Occasionally, such a stock will violate the prior support. In this instance, you are probably better off selling the stock for a small loss. But more likely, the long-term support will hold, meaning you just found yourself an excellent buying opportunity.

Should you identify such an opportunity and not buy the stock, don't panic. Instead, be patient and wait for the inevitable pullback off the up-trend. The lowest point you want to buy the stock is the 0.618 retrace. But typically, you can accomplish a low-cost buy at approximately a 40 to 50 percent pullback off the highs. Remember, by waiting for the 0.618 retrace price, you may miss the move entirely. Buying near the early retrace price makes a lot of sense because you are accumulating cheap shares at low risk. As with many low-priced stocks, you will find multiple opportunities to climb aboard a stock before its potential becomes widely known.

Many investors, understandably, find the best bargains at the bottom. They monitor the columns about stocks making new lows in the financial press and look for high-volume stocks that are often gapping down on panic selling. The best candidates are often found among the best-known names, which attract a lot of uninformed buying from investors who are prone to panic when things don't go their way. A recent example of just such a stock was the well-known California-based data storage specialist Iomega (IOM). See Figure 3.35.

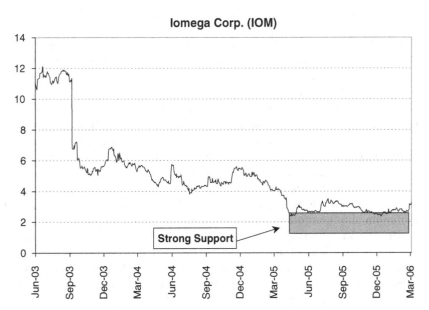

FIGURE 3.35 The Rise, Fall, and Rebound of Iomega

Iomega once enjoyed widespread popularity among tech traders. In March 2005, however, it began gapping down on high volume as investors panicked and sold Iomega shares indiscriminately. Within three days of the March gap (the rule of three), the stock stabilized at its lows, and it has since rallied approximately 33 percent. In such a situation, you must understand that the herd mentality, resulting in panicked selling, creates an opportunity for those who are not losing their heads. The fact that the stock has since bounced off those lows suggests the value of stepping in at the bottom.

The situation in Iomega is interesting to analyze. The gap down day in March created additional selling on the subsequent trading day and the day following that. After three days down, the market was ready to rally. The bottom was now intact, and after a period of consolidation, in which the support held, the stock slowly began to gain ground. It has since formed a strong support at the $2.50 level prior to what will probably be a strong rally.

When a strong base forms at a support level, you have a good indication that higher prices are in the offing. This is a strong indication of a low-risk buy because the general technical rule is that the more time a stock spends at a given price (going sideways), the stronger the subsequent move.

This pattern can occur at a bottom or virtually anywhere on the way up (after, say, an initial leg up). The one exception is at the top. You will rarely witness a stock that soars to new heights only to go sideways. Rather, tops typically occur quickly, followed by a sudden thrust down as longs head for the exits in a wholesale selling frenzy. Everyone wants to sell at the top, right? The only problem with this is that once it becomes widely known that the top has occurred, it is too late to casually exit. Selling begets selling, and you often have a fast break.

The antidote to finding yourself amid a crowd of sellers is to anticipate the top with what I call time-and-price calculations. But for now, let's continue our discussion of identifying the low-risk buying opportunity.

It should be clear by now that there are abundant areas where you can safely purchase a rising stock. Indeed, to go to absurd lengths, with some bullish stocks, you can buy them just about anywhere and make money. That's because they are headed higher in a serious way. But with most stocks, it pays to do a little homework and buy them when the risk is at a minimum and the profit potential is high. That's the ideal pattern. The less adversity you encourage, the more likely you won't do something stupid, like sell your shares on a temporary break. You'd be surprised how often this precise scenario takes place. Moreover, since Murphy's Law tends to rule, chances are you will compound your mistake with another one. In the financial markets, Murphy was always considered an optimist.

One notion you want to entertain is to buy at long-standing support levels or on breakouts. When I say support levels, I also mean trendlines, for these likewise are support levels, albeit at slightly higher prices. The higher-risk strategy is clearly the buying of the breakout. A breakout that doesn't run could signal a major trend reversal. The lower-risk strategy involves a bit more patience. Wait until you see a significant uptrend; then buy the stock on the pullback. A third strategy involves being a bottom-fisher. But this one, too, is fraught with danger. What if the bottom you're fishing isn't the actual bottom but a rest stop on the way to significantly lower prices? You may be in for a rude surprise.

A well-respected pattern is the stair-step configuration formed on the charts when a strong stock powers its way higher. Sharply up is followed by sideways to down; draw in the vertical and horizontal lines on the charts and you'll find a virtual blueprint to higher prices.

Abraxas Petroleum (ABP) recently surged over $9. See Figure 3.36. This was a stock for which I had paid less than $1.50 just 15 months ago. More recently it tripled in value from $3 to $9. The stock was a breakout play the entire trip higher. Once it met resistance at $5 a share, many investors probably thought the move was over because they offered it down to under $4.50. But on the next leg up, it broke the resistance at $5 and

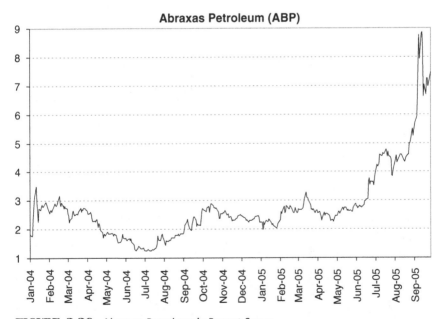

FIGURE 3.36 Abraxas Petroleum's Recent Surge

traded up to $9 in just 10 trading days. What a dramatic move! Last year no one had heard of this stock. Now that it has risen approximately 1,000 percent in value, the stock is featured on CNBC. While the serious money has already been made here, the point is clear: Buying breakouts can be extremely profitable.

For those of us who prefer a little less risk, you can always look to purchase the countermove down following a sharp rise. Even a casual glance at some price charts will reveal stocks trending higher in this fashion. Whether you want to track high-volume stocks or percent gainers (they are often the same stocks), you will find an abundance of likely candidates. Tracking average versus recent one-day high-volume statistics will also yield a list of likely candidates. I own a stock that typically trades approximately a-million shares a day. It recently experienced one-day volume of 7 million shares—seven times the normal volume. This was a clue that the stock was getting ready to run.

A recent example of a stock breaking new volume and percentage gains is JDSU. See Figure 3.37. While I've never owned this stock, it has interested me as a follower of troubled companies. For a long time, this was a stock without a bottom. Now the tables have turned. After months basing at the $1.50 a share level, the stock gained 60 percent in value in just three weeks!

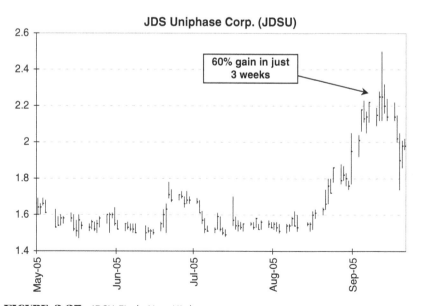

FIGURE 3.37 JDSU Finds New Highs

If you want to see the classic low-risk buying opportunities, look at a recent chart of Spherion Corp. (SFN). See Figure 3.38. The stock made a clear-cut trend from $5 to $8 per share before the countermove drove it back to the $7 level, where it found support. With much of the trading at approximately $7.50 a share, the stock is poised to break out above $8 trading up or over $10, where it will undoubtedly meet some near-term resistance. There are many similar examples of low-risk buying opportunities. The key is finding the initial trend and then identifying the countermove down, prior to purchasing the shares within the support area.

The ultimate signal that a stock is ripe for a strong rally is when the stock makes a one-day new low and closes at the top of the day's range. This means the last seller has given up and thrown in the towel. Bargain hunters see this capitulation as the sign that the stock is poised to move higher. The speed with which the bottom is made is the confirmation of the uptrend. Typically, this happens only after a prolonged period of declining prices and general malaise in the stock. The bottom is usually the point where all hope has been lost.

The term *support* is thrown around by technical analysts as if it had a single meaning. But there is short- and long-term support and intermediate support in between. Newspapers are quick to report 52-week highs and lows because these two prices sum up a year's worth of resistance and

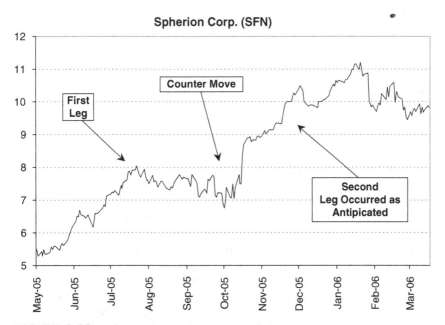

FIGURE 3.38 Spherion Corp.: Classic Low-Risk Opportunity

support. But support can be a one- or two-day affair, or it can persist for weeks and hold despite numerous selling campaigns to send prices lower. The simplest and perhaps most useful concept involving support and resistance is that once violated, one becomes the other, and vice versa. The most obvious way to utilize this concept is to know that you might want to purchase at the support, but if it is broken, you may want to become a seller at the old support—which is now the overhead resistance!

Stocks tend to gravitate toward specific prices. When a stock trades at a support price, it often means that both sellers and buyers are comfortable with that price, given the current circumstances of the company. The springboard for higher or lower prices, therefore, will typically be bullish or bearish news. Given one or the other, the stock will then break or run higher.

Ideally, you would always buy at the bottom and sell at the top. But this is not going to happen. The idea is to make money, not become perfect in picking tops and bottoms. The extremes, of course, are never known in advance, only in hindsight. What may indeed prove to be a 10-year low in a stock may, at the time it was occurring, look like the spot where there is no bottom—the spot where the buyer feels like the stock price is the proverbial hot knife cutting through butter. So give yourself a break when you are thinking about purchasing a stock. The lowest-risk opportunity (buying at the ultimate bottom) is now gone. You'll have to settle for purchasing on a breakout or intermediate countermove off a rally. This may be the best risk-to-reward ratio you can find. Put another way, the real bottom is unknowable; the challenge is to decipher the direction of the move and jump on before too much of the rally is already gone.

One easy method of figuring where *not* to buy a stock is when the stock has already made a gigantic move. When you are near or at the bottom, you will find no discussion of the stock, either in the financial press or among the gurus on CNBC. Once the stock registers some impressive percentage gains, however, it inevitably attracts attention. That's the time to sell it if you already own it.

As I mentioned before, I heard my Abraxas Petroleum shares talked about on CNBC the other day. That's the first time in almost two years I'd ever heard the stock's name in public. Why? Perhaps that's because it has recently traded near $9 a share. Several years ago, the stock traded under $1 a share. Moreover, the volume in recent days has been 10 times the normal volume. High volume can be a clue that a stock is about to run. But in this case, it probably means a significant short-term top has been established. I wish I could say that I'd ridden the stock to the $9 level. But the fact is I'd long since taken profits and moved on to other opportunities. Looking back on this investment, it gives me great satisfaction to know that I discovered this hidden gem, even if I didn't recognize its enormous potential at the time. Clearly, this was a stock that got away.

Next, as we attempt to refine our selection process for finding a good low-priced stock, we will look at the most critical component of stock selection, timing. Good timing is what separates today's winning selection from tomorrow's dog. Fortunately, there is a wealth of research available to tell us the best time to buy and sell stocks.

Timing

V ince Lombardi, the legendary coach of the Green Bay Packers, once commented that winning isn't the most important thing, it's the only thing! In the market, the same could be said about timing. Even a casual glance at just about any stock chart will clearly illustrate, in retrospect, the best place to buy and sell a stock. Take the case of Taser International, the manufacturer of the popular stun gun. Taser was once a penny stock. It later soared to $30 a share—twice! Following the first rise, it retreated to $15 a share. Following the second rise, it retreated to $5 a share. Looking back, depending on where you bought Taser stock, you could have made—or lost—substantial sums of money. Believe me, impressive fortunes were made in this former high-flying penny stock.

Put another way, it was all a matter of timing.

There are clear-cut cycles in the market that pinpoint where the overall market—and, to a lesser extent, individual stocks—should be purchased and sold. Actually, to complicate matters a little, there are crosscurrents of cycles that often correspond to one another. You would be surprised how often the general rules apply to specific stocks.

For starters, there is the saying that a rising tide lifts all boats. In a bull market, therefore, even lackluster stocks experience higher prices. The same, no doubt, is likewise true for declining markets. But the general guidelines for specific cyclical patterns are so reliable that just about every investor should be familiar with the market's so-called seasonality.

SEASONALITY

The notion of seasonality in the stock market arose from the well-known cyclical patterns that originally occurred in the agricultural markets. Crops were traditionally planted in the spring and harvested in the fall, in the process creating periods of scarcity and abundance. When the crops were growing, prices for agricultural commodities tended to be high; at harvest time, with winter approaching, the crop came to market in great abundance, resulting in seasonal lows in crop prices. Indeed, this very cyclical pattern in agricultural commodities created the need for the futures markets, which enabled both growers and processors of raw commodities to offset their risks.

Given this background, you wouldn't think that the stock market would demonstrate similar seasonal tendencies. But the cyclical patterns in stock prices are both pronounced and reliable over many years. There are reasons why the securities markets are cyclical in nature. For one, tax selling and window dressing among the influential institutional players tend to create periods when stocks are weak relative to other times of the year. For another, the year of the presidential cycle is another important variable in selecting the best time to purchase stock. Let's turn now to the most reliable patterns and see whether they will prove helpful in our stock selection process.

Glance at a chart of average stock prices over a period of years, and you will see that September and October tend to be periods of depressed prices, whereas market highs tend to be registered in late January through early April. In Figure 4.1, this seasonal tendency for stock prices is clearly indicated.

October has traditionally been among the weakest months of the year for stock prices. Think of the stock market crashes in both October 1929 and, 58 years later, in October 1987. After the terrorist attack in September 2001, the stock market also made a significant low in this September-October period. The good news about this market drop is that the market staged significant rallies following these market breaks.

Just as fall is notable as a period when stocks are weak, early winter is known as a period of strong stock prices. Witness the so-called January effect, which suggests that stocks are traditionally strong in late January after weakness during the prior fall. Moreover, the evidence suggests that low-priced stocks are among the strongest contenders for price appreciation during this period.

In studies that have gone back more than 70 years, this January effect has proven a reliable indicator for security prices. During the first month of the year, investors get serious about making money (as opposed to

FIGURE 4.1 S&P 500 Index Seasonal Tendencies

December, when their attention is more on spending money for consumer goods). Another viewpoint suggests that institutions receive large contributions during December and their investment of these funds serves to push stock prices higher in January. Still others suggest that markets are flush with money in the final days of one month and the early days of the next month and that this abundance of capital is why stocks receive a boost.

Cyclical studies demonstrate that stocks are cyclical not only on a seasonal basis but also on a day-of-the-week basis, and even within a given trading day. I know that this is really fine-tuning, but wouldn't you prefer to know that early Monday morning is an excellent time to purchase a stock rather than Thursday morning, when, following a week of strong prices, the market is poised to break lower? The evidence suggests that Monday is probably the strongest day of the week and that Thursday is overwhelmingly the weakest day of the week. While these are generalities, they are precisely the kind of information that can give you an important edge. There are even significant seasonal patterns related to holidays.

Look at the chart for Hemispherx BioPharma (HEB) in Figure 4.2. The company's stock staged an impressive rally off the September–October lows, doubling in price.

The widely traded JDSU shows the top in January and the bottom just prior to the rally in October. Sell in January, and buy in October. See Figure 4.3.

Another example of this seasonal pattern is displayed by Starbucks Corp., shown in Figure 4.4.

And Covad Communications Group (DVW) in Figure 4.5 illustrates a strong seasonal trend, allowing you to buy in October and sell in January to capitalize on this market cycle.

With so many institutional and individual investors willing to take losses in December (in order to lessen their April tax bills), it shouldn't come as any surprise that January is an excellent time for stocks to rise. When institutional investors sell just prior to the end of a quarter (or, as in this case, a tax year), the phenomenon is known as window dressing. By realizing the losses, the losing investments don't appear as paper losses on the fund's books. All this selling, of course, has a pronounced negative impact on prices. Selling begets selling, as sell stops are triggered. And pretty soon, you have a situation where share prices are pushed to bargain-basement levels. After the first of the month (or year), you then have the

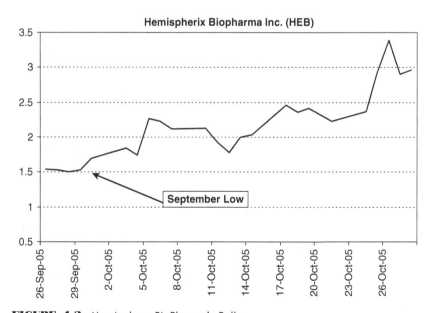

FIGURE 4.2 Hemispherx BioPharma's Rally

FIGURE 4.3 JDSU's Top and Bottom

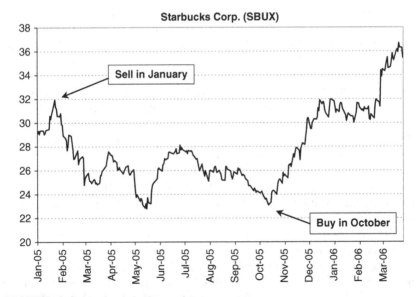

FIGURE 4.4 Starbucks's Top and Bottom

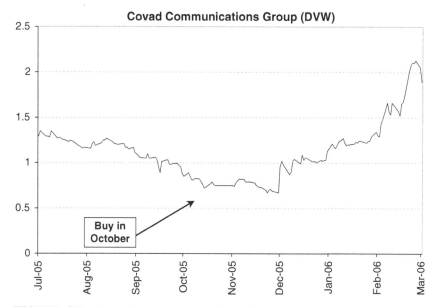

FIGURE 4.5 Covad Communications Group Shows a Strong Seasonal Trend

reverse phenomenon. With the IRS-related selling pressure gone, the market is free to rise on new buying—hence, the so-called January effect.

There is also a cash-flow theory that proposes another reason for the seasonality of stock markets. In January, new money in the form of end-of-year bonuses or pension plan contributions can provide another impetus for higher prices. With the move toward more and more institutional players in the market, the January effect has become even more pronounced in recent years. This institutional impact also plays a role in why October is traditionally such a weak month. October 31 has increasingly become the deadline for tax-related selling for those institutional players who plan to make year-end capital gains distributions to their shareholders.

More than a few Wall Street analysts have, over the years, pointed out the viability of buying in the late fall and selling after the first of the year. Moreover, the statistics tend to confirm this assertion, especially among low- and depressed-price stocks. The small stocks have an impressive gain of almost 7 percent over this period of time, compared to gains of just 1.5 percent for the larger stocks.

One rule: Don't wait for confirmation prior to buying. These low-priced opportunities are available only briefly. Within weeks of making their 52-week lows, these stocks often make impressive gains. Obviously, once a stock makes an important rise, it is no longer the bargain it once was.

You want to buy stocks by mid-December at the latest—and often the best prices are found as early as middle-to-late October. You can then sell in January or hold the position beyond that point, and know that you availed yourself of the best possible seasonal buying pattern.

You don't want to be left behind in capitalizing on seasonal patterns. On the other hand, you don't want to purchase too soon, lest you find yourself averaging down in a declining market. Ideally, you want to discover a tightly coiled stock ready to spring higher. As you can imagine, good timing is the key to buying at the right level. When you're looking at a seasonal opportunity, timing is everything.

Studies also suggest that a leading stock market index, the Standard & Poor's 500, tends to demonstrate consistent patterns on a seasonal basis. In early January, just prior to the rising prices we call the January effect, prices tend to decline for a week or two. This is typically followed by rising prices into March. Later in the summer, look for a lull from August through October. The most reliable seasonal pattern in the S&P 500 then occurs as prices consistently rise in November and December. Indeed, they may start rising as soon as October. Here's a list of the most prominent patterns to consider:

- Lows the first week in January
- Highs in March
- Secondary highs in August
- Lows in October or November
- Highs into the end of the year

HOW TO USE THE BULLISH CONSENSUS WITH SEASONAL PATTERNS

For almost 40 years now, several firms have attempted to measure the relative bullishness of the stock market by publishing weekly Bullish Consensus numbers. Market Vane, a company based in Pasadena, California, pioneered the idea of taking a weekly survey of select market participants and trying to come up with a single percentage that reflected their thinking. In general, a high number (above 70 percent) suggests bullishness; a low number (under 30 percent) suggests bearishness. The idea, however, was to use the numbers as a so-called contrary indicator; that is, high bullishness often signaled the market was overbought, and high bearishness signaled the reverse, an oversold market. The reasoning was that if so many participants were bullish, the market had nowhere to go except down. Likewise, with the predominant crowd of investors bearish, the market, went the thinking, was for ripe for a sharp rally. When the degree of bullish or bearish sentiment fell in the middle, however, the readings were decidedly mixed. To use contrary indicators, you clearly want an overwhelming majority on one side or the other.

One way to time the market on a seasonal basis, therefore, is to use the Bullish Consensus as a contrary indicator in conjunction with seasonal patterns. Remember, the hallmark of contrary opinion theory is that the crowd is typically wrong at the major turns. So let's assume for a minute that we are considering a seasonal trade in a particular stock, but we want to refine our timing skills by looking at a confirming indicator.

Because October is almost always a weak month in terms of stock prices, let's assume we are looking to buy XYZ stock. A glance at the stock tables tells us what we undoubtedly already know: XYZ is trading at, let's say, $3 having had a 52-week range of $8 on the high and $2 on the low. Clearly, the stock had been beaten down. To further refine our strategy, we might look at the Bullish Consensus numbers for the stock market as a whole. Let's say the percentages are close to the bottom, below 10 percent. It's October, the weakest month of the year, and the news is primarily bearish—so bearish, in fact, that 90 percent of investors see the market going lower and only 10 percent anticipate higher prices in the months ahead. Believe it or not, this is an ideal buying opportunity!

When the last seller has sold, the low has been reached. A conformation of the reverse in the trend is a *rise* in the Bullish Consensus. So after observing a reading under 10 percent, let's say investors become a little more bullish (but still very bearish) as the percentages rise to, say, 15 percent. This is the signal to buy.

Here are some rules:

- By the first Friday of October, the Bullish Consensus must be at or below 40 percent—and it must be a lower number than the week before.
- On or before November 30, the Bullish Consensus must be a higher number than the week before.
- Buy as soon as you see this change in the trend of the Bullish Consensus numbers.

HOW TO CONSTRUCT AN OSCILLATOR

An oscillator, which is defined as a means of measuring different fluctuating values, is among the most reliable indicators of market strength. While subject to interpretation, the oscillator will give you a reading to judge a stock's relative strength or weakness. There are many different types of oscillators that measure relative market strength, and we will cover several here. Rest assured that an oscillator reading is among the best timing tools that market professionals rely on in selecting stocks to buy and sell.

The 5-Day Oscillator

You want to know, in the early stages, when a stock is poised to move higher. This oscillator generates a reading that will clearly tell you whether the stock is bullish or bearish. It generates a number between 0 and 100. Typically, readings above 70 are considered bullish, and readings below 30 are considered bearish. Readings between 30 and 70 are considered neutral.

Because the oscillator is based on five days of data, the reading pinpoints near-term strength or weakness. Once you have a series of readings, you can draw a line connecting them to show when the stock becomes a good buy or sell.

The formula for the oscillator is as follows:

Highest price in last 5 days − Open 5 days = X

Last close − Lowest price in last 5 days = Y

$$\frac{(\mathbf{X} + \mathbf{Y}) \times \mathbf{100}}{(\textbf{Highest price in last 5 days} - \textbf{Lowest Price in last 5 days}) \times \mathbf{2}}$$

At this point, generating the reading becomes just a matter of doing the calculations. Consider the recent data for JDSU prices:

Day	Open	High	Low	Close
1	2.00	2.02	1.96	1.98
2	1.91	2.01	1.86	1.98
3	2.01	2.05	1.74	1.90
4	2.15	2.15	2.00	2.02
5	2.15	2.22	2.12	2.14

The calculations would appear as follows:

(highest price) − 2.15 (open 5 days back) = .07 = X

(last close) − 1.74 (lowest low in 5 days = .24 = Y

$$\frac{.31(X + Y) \times 100 \ = \ 31}{(2.22\ [\text{highest price}] - 1.74\ [\text{lowest price}]\ = \ .48) \times 2} = 32\%$$

The oscillator reading is 32 percent, meaning tomorrow's reading is neutral since it falls between 30 and 70 percent.

The 3-Day Difference in the 5-Day Oscillator

Once you understand how to calculate the 5-day oscillator, you want to begin collecting the readings in order to create the 3-day difference number. This value represents the speed and direction of the 5-day oscillator. A positive number indicates the oscillator is moving up (positive momentum), and a negative number indicates the oscillator is moving down (negative momentum). A large number indicates the oscillator is moving too fast and the market may be setting up for a reversal. The formula is as follows:

Current value of the 5-day oscillator − Value of the oscillator 3 days ago

= 3-day difference

Consider the following values:

Day	5-Day Oscillator Reading	3-Day Difference
1	32	−35
2	20	−70
3	63	
4	67	
5	90	

The readings are becoming less negative (or more positive), suggesting the stock is nearing a bottom and is about to rally higher.

Pivot Breakout Numbers

There are both buy and sell pivot breakout numbers. In the case of the pivot breakout buy, the formula calculates a price above the previous close that represents a level at which the market is breaking to new highs; in the case of the pivot sell, the formula calculates a price below the previous close at which the market is considered to be breaking lower. The two formulas are as follows:

$$\frac{(\text{Day's high} + \text{Day's low} + \text{Day's close})}{3} = X$$

$$2X - \text{Day's low} = \text{Pivot Breakout Buy Number}$$

$$\frac{(\text{Day's high} + \text{Day's low} + \text{Day's close})}{3} = X$$

$$2X - \text{Day's high} = \text{Pivot Breakout Sell Number}$$

Now, assume the following:

High $= 7.62$

Low $= 7.26$

Close $= 7.46$

The pivot buy and sell numbers would be as follows:

$$\frac{7.62 + 7.26 + 7.46}{3} = 7.45 = X$$

$14.90(2X) - 7.26\,(\text{day's low}) = 7.64 = \text{Pivot Breakout Buy}$

$14.90(2X) - 7.62\,(\text{day's high}) = 7.28 = \text{Pivot Breakout Sell}$

The 1-Day Strength Indicator

This formula measures how the stock closed on the day. The formula generates a number between 0 and 100, suggesting the higher the number, the stronger the close. It is assumed that a strong close means higher prices ahead.

The 1-day strength indicator formula is as follows:

$$\frac{(\text{close} - \text{low})}{(\text{high} - \text{low})} \times 100$$

Assume the following:

High $= 7.20$

Low $= 6.65$

Close $= 7.08$

The calculations:

$$\frac{7.08\,(\text{close}) - 6.65\,(\text{low}) = 0.43 \times 100 = 43}{7.20\,(\text{high}) - 6.65\,(\text{low})} = 78\%$$

This number suggests the stock closed strong since it was in the higher percentile of the range.

While we like to buy stocks that demonstrate strength as measured by the 1-day strength index, this valuable indicator can also pinpoint climax selling days. These are days when the selling is so overwhelming that the inevitable bounce back up is almost a certainty. The best way to identify a selling climax is when the 1-day strength number falls under 25 percent.

The lower the number, of course, the more oversold the market. This, naturally, means the stock has now experienced its lows and is indeed headed higher.

In summary, the 5-day oscillator is used to identify the trend. The 1-day strength indicator is used to fine-tune the entry price. The buy and sell pivotal numbers can likewise point to a good entry. And the 3-day difference in the 5-day oscillator can tell you at what point you are in a trading cycle, making your entry or exit selection as low-risk as possible.

MOMENTUM ANALYSIS

Oscillators, as you can see, are useful in analyzing the rate at which markets rise and fall. Momentum players are quick to jump aboard a stock that may be entering its initial surge higher—but equally quick to abandon this position once the stock shows signs of slowing at the top. They are short-term investors who believe that speed and agility are key to maximizing profits. They want to be in the market early and out long before their fellows recognize the party may be over.

Momentum is strictly a matter of degree and timing. If the momentum player is a day late, the entire strategy may be destroyed. The momentum player must understand oscillator readings and how to interpret them. To such an investor, high volume, demonstrating wide participation, is essential for the good opportunity. They move from stock to stock, always seeking the hot stock at the right time.

Momentum players are also known as swing traders, because they attempt to catch temporary price swings. They understand that momentum is a matter of degree. A stock may be forming a well-known saucer pattern, or cup and handle. Once the prices start forming the handle portion of the pattern, they are ready to jump on the stock at the first sign of a breakout signaling higher prices. If you think being a momentum player is easy, think again. Not every chart pattern pans out. And when a formation fails, chances are an army of like-minded investors are all heading to the exits at the same time, resulting in substantial losses. Momentum analysis is the high-wire act of the investment world. It is not for the faint of heart.

Momentum players are always asking themselves what ought to happen. A market drifts lower, and pretty soon there is wholesale selling, which should cause prices to fall even further. Their opportunity comes when the predictable doesn't occur. That's when they spot their hard-won opportunity.

TRADING FILTERS

As the name suggests, trading filters are used to filter out the less favorable opportunities, allowing you to concentrate on those stocks most likely to return handsome profits. Understandably, pinpointing the winners is often a daunting task. Stocks can trade in the doldrums for months before making a substantial move, and filters help you get the edge in identifying the best buying candidates.

What is a filter? A filter can be virtually any rule that tells you to leave one investment alone while perhaps looking for another. They can be simple rules or complicated strategies involving three or four codependent indicators all pointing in a single direction. Some filters have to do with so-called day-of-the-week strategies, in which better buying opportunities exist during certain days of the week. Others have to do with recent price action. Do you really, for example, want to buy a stock on the third day up? Ample research suggests that this is perhaps not the best strategy.

I like to buy stocks on Monday, especially early in the day, because Monday is a particularly strong day in the stock market. But the filter I use is to limit my buys to Mondays following relatively weak Fridays. This can be measured by the performance of the stock market as a whole (by looking at the averages) or by monitoring the particular stock. When my 1-day strength index of a stock I am monitoring is low on a Friday, I'm more inclined to purchase on the following Monday morning. This is because the statistics favor such a move.

Moving ahead on the week, you don't want to buy on a Tuesday following a barn-burning Monday. Why? Because Monday morning's bargain may be Tuesday's overpriced stock. So unless my stock closes in the lower 25 percent of the day's range on a Monday, as measured by the 1-day strength reading, I'm going to leave it alone on Tuesday. A weak Monday, of course, may mean a strong close on Tuesday. So that's what I'm looking for in using this filter. In addition to the 1-day performance of your stock, you want to track the 5-day performance to get a clue as to where it is in the trading cycle. If I am looking to buy on a Tuesday, I want the 5-day oscillator to be below 50 percent. Again, this is because I want to buy before the rally occurs—not at the top of the rally. Understandably, a high 5-day oscillator reading suggests the stock has already made a strong up move, if only momentarily.

As the week progresses, I may put off buying until Wednesday. But I want to use my filters to alert me to a good buy versus a reckless buy. If the stock hasn't moved yet, I want to buy it. A quick calculation of the 1-day strength will tell me where it closed on Tuesday. If it closed above 12.5 percent, I want to leave it alone. Consider for a minute what a high percentage reading would mean. A high strength reading says the stock closed near the highs of the day. This means early buyers are now sitting on profits. Those with a short-term orientation will probably become sellers. This, in turn, will drive the price lower. The same strategies apply to buying on Thursdays and Fridays. If the stock is trading near its highs on the end of the prior day, chances are the best buying opportunity has passed. The stock is vulnerable to a selloff, and you need to be careful. This is just one simple way of using a single filter to find the best buying opportunities.

Here's a brief summary of the rules for buying on specific days of the week:

Day of the Week	1-Day Strength Index Percent
Monday	Less than 10
Tuesday	Less than 25
Wednesday	Less than 12.5
Thursday	Less than 14
Friday	Less than 17.5

Now let's look at the larger cyclical picture by using the 5-day oscillator. This oscillator tells you where, within the bull and bear cycle, the stock trades based on the previous 5 days' of price action. Unlike the 1-day strength indicator, which measures just yesterday's price action, the 5-day oscillator looks at a larger picture.

With the exception of Monday, the overwhelmingly best day to purchase stocks, you want to limit your buys to days when the 5-day oscillator is under 50 percent and, under most circumstances, to readings of less than 42 percent. The sole exception is Friday, when buying strength is the way to go in anticipation of a truly strong upward move on the subsequent Monday. Here are the rules for buying on specific days of the week in terms of the 5-day oscillator readings:

Day of the Week	5-Day Oscillator Percent
Monday	Buy at any reading
Tuesday	Less than 50
Wednesday	Less than 42
Thursday	Less than 42
Friday	Greater than 42

Another buying rule is to purchase at the prior day's lows. The reason for this rule is simple: That's where the support exists. There's a good (although not certain) chance that prices will stabilize at yesterday's lows. This is just one simple filter that can stand you in good stead for making sound buying decisions.

The reason that so many investors lose money in the market is that they don't have the discipline to use filters of any kind. They simply want to buy and hope for the best. This buying, understandably, often takes place amid a crowd of like-minded buyers. This means they end up buying the top. Moreover, they don't have a clue as to why they purchased when they did.

One sure sign of this mindless buying occurs in anticipation of earnings reports. Typically, stocks are bid up in anticipation of the report. More often than not, the report, even if good, doesn't measure up to the unrealistic expectations of the crowd, and there is a rush to the exits. This wholesale selling generates many, many losses among investors. More often than not, the stock price then stages a rally and trades higher. By utilizing even a few good filters, average investors can save themselves from falling victim to their own lack of discipline.

As a general rule, markets get out of line. By that, I mean they often go up too fast and they likewise often break too fast. This rapid price movement is generated, of course, by emotional investors who either don't want to miss a move or who want out at all costs. As a result, you get panicked moves that have no rhyme or reason in terms of the underlying fundamentals of the individual stock. The way to both avoid becoming a victim of this panic and capitalize on the situation is to try to understand the underlying phenomenon taking place.

We've already mentioned that stocks tend to experience selling climaxes when they reach a bottom. This is because the final long (buyer) has sold and is glad to be rid of the stock. Ironically, this selling climax is among the strongest possible buying signals you can have. When everyone else is losing their wits, you should be taking the attitude that you won't panic and that bargain-basement-priced shares are exactly what you are looking for. A selling climax ends with the market closing in the lower portion of the day's range. You may have a so-called key reversal day with the close at the top, but this is relatively rare. Instead, you have a situation where shares are being pushed lower by hopeless longs. This very hopelessness is the key that a buying opportunity exists.

An intelligent way to approach this problem is to *quantify* the market despair or enthusiasm in terms of a number. The 1-day strength and 5-day oscillator readings provide you with such a number. You then have to ignore your emotions and buy the stock based on the probabilities favoring the best outcome.

The value of learning to quantify price action—by using filters—is perhaps best illustrated by looking at an example. In the table that follows, I've listed several days of stock prices for 3M Co. (MMM), the well-known maker of Scotch tape, Post-it notes, and a range of industrial products. While definitely not a low-price stock, 3M recently made new lows just prior to issuing positive guidance for a 10 percent rise in profits in the coming months. After taking out the prior lows, the stock found support just before soaring higher, a truly classic move. On a technical basis, the key to the move was hidden in the daily range statistics. Here they are:

Day	Date	Open	High	Low	Close
1	Mon. Oct 17	71.01	72.69	70.78	72.47
2	Fri. Oct 14	70.28	70.78	70.08	70.72
3	Thurs. Oct 13	70.11	70.88	69.71	70.07
4	Wed. Oct 12	70.29	71.25	70.15	70.38
5	Tues. Oct 11	71.25	71.30	70.35	70.55
6	Mon. Oct 10	72.00	72.20	71.26	71.39
7	Fri. Oct 7	71.51	71.99	71.27	71.73
8	Thurs. Oct 6	71.36	71.77	70.49	71.11
9	Wed. Oct 5	71.41	71.93	71.15	71.17

First, let's do the calculations for the 5-day oscillator. Because you need five days of data to do the calculations, the first reading won't occur until day 4, Wednesday, October 12. For purposes of illustration, we will work through the numbers for day 4 and then just record the reading for day 3 through day 1. Accordingly, the 5-day oscillator for day 4 would be calculated as follows:

$$72.20 \text{ (highest price)} - 71.41 \text{ (open 5 days back)} = 0.79 = X$$

$$70.55 \text{ (last close)} - 70.35 \text{ (lowest low in 5 days)} = 0.20 = Y$$

$$\frac{0.99 \ (X + Y) \times 100 = 99}{(72.20 \ [\text{highest price}] - 70.35 \ [\text{lowest price}] = 1.85) \times 2} = 27\%$$

Thus, the 5-day oscillator at the beginning of day 4 is 27 percent. The table below shows the 5-day oscillator reading for days 1 through 4:

Day	Date	5-Day Oscillator Reading
1	Mon. Oct 17	10%
2	Fri. Oct 14	21%
3	Thurs. Oct 13	26%
4	Wed. Oct. 12	27%

By the time the oscillator reaches its lowest reading—10%—the bottom has already been reached (on Thursday, October 13), and the market is clearly headed higher. Indeed, by day 0—Tuesday, October 18—MMM shares traded as high as 79.39, $5.68 above its prior Thursday lows. Thursday is traditionally the weakest day of the week. In this instance, the general rule proved to be entirely correct. Looking back at the 5-day percent readings, all 4 days listed would have proved rewarding to buyers of MMM shares.

Now let's look at 1-day strength index percentages to see whether any one day would have proved a better buy than another. For purposes of illustration, we will do the calculations on day 1 and then list the results for days 1 through 4.

The reading for Monday, October 17, is based on the results of the previous day, Friday, October 14. The day's range on Friday was as follows:

Open = 70.28

High = 70.78

Low = 70.08

Close = 70.72

The calculations are as follows:

$$\frac{(70.72\,[\text{previous close}] - 70.08\,[\text{previous low}]) \times 100}{70.78\,(\text{previous high}) - 70.08\,(\text{previous low})} = 64/70 = 91\%$$

The readings for all 4 days would appear as follows:

Day	Date	1-Day Strength Percent
1	Mon. Oct 17	91%
2	Fri. Oct 14	31%
3	Thurs. Oct 13	21%
4	Wed. Oct 12	21%

Looking ahead, using the results of Monday, October 17, the 1-day strength reading for Tuesday, October 18, would be 88 percent. Tuesday proved to be another strong day for MMM, with the shares moving up another 3 percent to 74.65 at the close.

Based on the 1-day index strength numbers, none of the days proved weak enough to signal a strong oversold condition. But if you go back to Wednesday, October 5, you can see that the 1-day strength index was only 2 percent on that day, signaling a buy on the following day, Thursday, October 6. This signal would have gotten you in the market more than a week before the final lows and the substantial move higher.

STOPS

Stops—or stop-loss orders—are no less an important timing tool than those designed to fine-tune your entry into the market. Knowing how to enter the market is only half of the profitable equation. You must also know how to exit the market. Remember Martha Stewart's claim that she told her broker to sell ImClone stock when—and if—it hit 60? Stops are designed to minimize trading losses or to take profits when the market falls back. They are a common tool in any investor's list of strategies. The question becomes, however, how do you select a good spot to place a stop? Most analysts will admit that, when it comes to placing stops, you are on the horns of a dilemma. On the one hand, if the stock is placed too close to the current market price, a momentary break in prices will have you selling near a short-term low. On the other, if the stop is placed too far away from the market price, you will have lost too much money in the event the stop is indeed triggered. Although there is no easy solution to this problem, there are some guidelines you might want to follow.

First, you don't want to guess where to place the stop. A better approach is to take a 5-day average of the stock's range. To calculate this number is simplicity itself: Take the last five days of your stock's range, add them up, and divide by five. That is the average range for the last five trading days. Now you know, on average, what to expect in terms of the range. You then take 50 percent of that range and you place the stop for that amount below the low of the day.

By using this simple rule, you will minimize your losses when you initiate a position. Occasionally, the stop will be hit, and you will exit the market with a small loss. More often, the stop won't be hit, and you'll find you have entered into a profitable situation with minimal risk.

As your stock begins to trend higher, you want to place what are known as trailing stops. These are stops that trail the price higher. The idea is to always raise the stop and never lower it. Sooner or later, the stock will break the trendline, and you will exit the position with a profit. The rule is that the trailing stop should be approximately 65 percent of the 5-day range. The difference between a regular stop and a trailing stop is that the former is constant, whereas the latter will move higher with the stop. Because stops are typically entered on a day-only basis, you want to stay on top of your stop orders. So-called resting stop orders remain permanent. The drawback with this type of stop, however, is that investors often forget about them. Sometimes weeks or months later, their brokerage house will indicate that they sold a stock that they may no longer own. If you use resting orders, it is imperative that you maintain good records. Another approach to stop placement requires first-rate discipline: mental stops. This means you want to exit a market at a given price, but you do not actually place the stop order with your brokerage firm. Rather, you simply keep the idea in your head. Keep in mind the pitfalls of this strategy. You can forget your mental stops. Or you might decide to just watch the market, should the mental stop be hit. Failure to take action can result in substantial losses as you watch a stock's price deteriorate and do nothing. Disciplined traders, of course, know themselves well enough to take the profits—or losses—and exit the market according to the original plan.

MOVING AVERAGES

As a timing tool, moving averages tend to be lagging indicators. That means they follow market action, making you late buying or selling. A moving average is comprised of a number of closing prices divided by the number of days. An average is created when a series of numbers is summed and then divided by as many as were added. A moving average plots an average as it changes over time, with each new point adding the newest information and dropping the oldest. Hence, you might have 5-, 10-, 50-, 100-, or 200-day moving averages running against your daily prices. The shorter-term averages tend to jump around more and be more volatile than the longer-term averages. Much is made of the direction in which one average crosses another average. Yet, regardless of how you interpret moving averages, by definition, they are always late in pinpointing the trend. For longer-term-oriented investors, who are unlikely to be scared out of their positions by temporary setbacks, this is not a problem. For shorter-term traders, however, who might indeed be shaken out should the moving average lines head south, a downturn in the averages could spell trouble.

Moving averages also work like trendlines. Prices may approach, say, the 200-day moving average, where they will stop. Thus, many investors see a market that remains above such an average as above the stock's support. The breaking of such an average, of course, can be problematic. A stock that cannot stay above such an average may be showing signs of weakness.

There is nothing magical in choosing one average over another. Suffice it to say, most investors use two averages (one long, one short) and run them as simple lines across their price charts. That gives them an opportunity to graphically view the relationship between stock price and moving average. Since you can have averages of any length, the longer-term ones tend to be more significant: A stock that stays above a longer-term average is probably doing well versus a comparison of a stock's price with, let's say, the last 5 trading days. A break in the 5-day moving average may not be significant.

Moving averages can give you an insight into value. If you buy a house for $180,000 and you then find an identical house down the street selling for $150,000, you may feel that you overpaid. Likewise, in a world of soaring fuel prices, you may remember a time when you could purchase gasoline for 35 cents a gallon. Today's bargain is tomorrow's overpriced luxury item.

The moving average, therefore, serves to keep you focused on the overall trend of rising or falling prices. It allows you to have a sense of continuity in terms of whether a stock is expensive or cheap in historical terms. The bottom line: It can dramatically improve your timing when it comes to buying or selling your stock at the best possible price.

The moving average can tell you when a stock is selling low relative to where it has recently been. It can tell you when a stock price is soaring relative to its average price (should you sell?). It can tell you when the short-term trend is higher (when the short-term average crosses the longer-term average in an upward direction). In general, stock prices are low when they are below moving averages. Moreover, an abundance of evidence suggests out-of-favor low-priced stocks offer the best bang for the buck when it comes to capturing significant profits. Thus, the moving average is a simple yardstick, a timing tool to be used with other indicators to make the best possible stock selection.

MARKET TIMING: PRO AND CON

In the interest of being comprehensive, you must understand that not everyone agrees that successful market timing is possible. The general rationale among those in the investment community who put forth this idea is, yes, stocks generally go up over time, but it is virtually impossible to fine-tune the buying and selling of specific securities. In fact, this concept has a wide and loyal following on Wall Street.

Why?

Because if stocks rise over time (and most do), every day is a good day to purchase shares. This is a sales pitch. Don't worry about the short term. The only thing that matters is the long term. Well, as the noted British economist John Maynard Keynes once said, "In the long run we are all dead!" You might want to think about this the next time a broker tries to pressure you into buying a stock. Numerous studies clearly demonstrate that well-timed purchases (namely, those made just prior to bull moves) do much better than simply buying stocks willy-nilly.

Another reason why this notion that you can't time the market enjoys widespread popularity is that most Wall Streeters won't take the time to learn the basic timing tools discussed here. Why work at investing in the market when you can simply guess and play the market? Their attitude is sort of like the slot-machine mentality you might find in Las Vegas. The fact is that the most successful investors often work the hardest.

Is it difficult and frustrating to try to time the market? You bet. But the results are worth the effort. Market timing suggests that there are indicators that can be interpreted to help you buy and sell. It implies that there are data whose successful interpretation will provide you with an idea, a very good idea, about when a stock is poised to rise or decline.

What moves the market every day is a great many buyers and sellers all interacting. In the aggregate, they are all involved in market timing, doing their level best to buy low and sell high. Because not everyone can be entirely successful all the time doesn't disqualify them as legitimate participants. At the heart of the matter is the notion of price. When is a price too high or too low? Price is the mechanism by which virtually all goods and services are exchanged. Doesn't it stand to reason that price will dictate when a stock becomes overly expensive or inexpensive? Doesn't it stand to reason that a high or low price for a stock can be determined by looking at dividends or earnings or book value or a half-dozen other factors? Indeed, price is king because it is the wisdom of the markets that establishes whether a stock is expensive or cheap.

In a sense, the market is always right. After all, investors have little choice but to accept the market value given to their stock. In the next chapter, we turn to a special segment of the market, the initial public offering (IPO), which often prices shares well below their intrinsic value in hopes of raising capital to propel the business. This trade-off, however, is not without its risks because an IPO typically has no trading history. Nevertheless, some of the most successful people on Wall Street swear by IPOs.

CHAPTER 5

IPOs

I have a friend who has made a career specializing in a single type of investment—initial public offerings. IPO investing is tailor-made for the small stock investor because so many new offerings come from companies just starting out. Such public offerings attract a special type of investor, the kind that doesn't mind taking on substantial risk in pursuit of equally substantial profits. The rule in investing is that risk is commensurate with reward. In other words, you don't grow rich buying T-bills. In the IPO world, the risk stems from lack of knowledge about a company; its track record may be thin, and its trading record is often nonexistent. To borrow from Charles Dickens, the IPO is the worst of all investments and the best of all investments. It all depends on your perspective—and your results.

In an IPO, the company is typically poised to ramp-up its operations and enjoy a growth spurt. The reason for the IPO is that the company wants to raise capital for an exciting venture of some sort—one so special that the company's owners are willing to give up equity for cash. Smart entrepreneurs, of course, keep a substantial portion of stock for themselves. That way, should the stock enjoy a surge in price after the IPO, they can become rich on rising share values. Not a few stock market fortunes have been earned in this fashion.

As with so many things in the investment world, the IPO is a trade-off for a small company. A privately held company is free to more or less do what it wants with its assets. A publicly held company, however, has obligations and restrictions placed on its activities by regulatory authorities. In return for being able to offer shares to the public, the public company must publish quarterly and annual sales and earnings results. It must follow strict rules set down by the Securities and Exchange Commission (SEC) regarding disclosure of the company's activities. And it may be subject to the scrutiny of the company's board of directors. It needs to hire independent auditors and attorneys to ensure that it complies with regulatory requirements. In short, going public is not something that any company takes lightly.

Why would an entrepreneur, who enjoys 100 percent of a thriving company, give up partial ownership via an IPO? The answer is very simple. Sometimes less is more. A smaller portion of the pie may be substantially more valuable to a CEO with the foresight to put the money raised in the IPO to good use. That's why the capital raised in the IPO cannot be used simply to line the pockets of company executives. It must be put to work in a productive fashion. Thus, an offering is often contemplated when company executives find themselves faced with the dilemma of wanting to take on a project but in need of capital to do so.

Wanting to grow the company via an influx of new funds, management must often make an important decision: Do they borrow the money or sell stock? One approach a company can take is to arrange private financing; another is to sell corporate bonds. Both have the pesky problem of having to repay the funds, however. In the meantime, the company has to pay interest on the loan. An alternative, of course, is to issue stock via an IPO. Should management then fall on its face, the shareholders lose out—not the company—because there is no obligation to ever repay them for their investment. By issuing shares, a company gives up equity in return for cash. For the investors, the payoff comes if the shares rise in value.

While IPOs are extremely popular among investors, there are also ways for companies to issue stock once they have already become public companies. They can issue more stock, known as secondary offerings. These offerings, too, provide much-needed capital to microcaps.

The drawback for the investor is that IPOs and secondary issues typically come with the least amount of information available to the investing public. At best, you are dependent on a legally required prospectus and a road show put on by the company to highlight its potential. Since many of these deals are arranged privately and are typically offered only to high-net-worth individuals, you may even have difficulty learning about an IPO. Corporate financing is often an insular world, and information about a potentially lucrative IPO is typically not available to the average investor. This is unfortunate because some of these offerings are true opportunities that shouldn't be missed. Nevertheless, as so often happens in the investment world, the rich get richer, buying and selling IPO shares.

Apart from disclosing in the prospectus accurate information regarding the use of the funds raised in an IPO, the company is under no obligation to perform to the satisfaction of shareholders. Even a cursory glance at virtually any prospectus for an IPO will reveal pages upon pages of disclaimers, put there, no doubt, by the company's attorneys. These disclaimers typically state that the company has no idea if the projects it undertakes will be successful. The disclaimers, therefore, state the risk of purchasing the IPO shares. The investor must be careful about investing in an IPO.

Not all IPOs are structured in the same manner. Some provide the company greater leeway in the use of the money raised. I once knew a couple of brothers, Ralph and Bill, who built up a very successful software company. Wanting to expand, they turned to public financing. In reading over the prospectus prior to the IPO, a friend remarked to me:

"This is a great deal," he said, adding, "for Ralph and Bill."

They were offering a very small portion of the company at a relatively high per-share price. Once public, the shares traded lower.

There's a saying in the market that you never really know a stock until you own it. So if you aren't careful, your newly acquired IPO shares might begin to resemble something less than a stellar investment. With a secondary offering, at least you might have a liquid market and a public history to rely on. But secondaries have their drawbacks, too. They can lose their liquidity once the excitement of the offering wears off, and without liquidity, to whom are you planning to sell?

THE BASICS

An IPO occurs when a private company first offers to sell its shares to the public. This can be an exciting event for both company management and investors. You want to invest in an IPO because it can offer an opportunity to purchase low-priced shares in a growing business. IPOs often outperform other companies because they offer an unknown opportunity at a very cheap price. The out-of-line low pricing may be due to lack of knowledge about the prospects for the company, the small size of the company, or its undercapitalization. The other side of the coin is, of course, the fact that these are all risk factors. The investor in IPOs is banking on a belief that the money raised will be put to good use, resulting in improved profits and rising share values.

Because the management of an IPO may be new to Wall Street, they may be inexperienced in dealing with analysts and investors and not understand the importance of getting their story told to the investment community. When it comes to secondary offerings, a company has to be concerned with the impact of dilution of its shares. The number of shares and timing of the sale of secondary shares is of critical importance in maintaining shareholder value. If too many shares are offered on a secondary issue, the overall price of the shares declines.

A secondary offering occurs when a company that is already public issues new shares. There are many reasons why a company might want to make such an offer. It may want to pay for future acquisitions or pay down debt. The impact on the share price may be influenced by the secondary issue, but there is no clear-cut way to ascertain in advance precisely what this impact will be. Stock analysts may make buy, sell, or hold recommendations on a particular stock, which undoubtedly affect price.

THE PUBLIC OFFERING PROCESS

Long before the small investor can purchase IPO shares, the underwriters of the stock go through a lengthy process of getting the shares ready for listing. First, the company announces its intention of selling shares to the public. Second, the underwriters attempt to put an initial pricing offer on the table. Prior to the announcement, of course, the company has probably interviewed several underwriters, which are typically large brokerage firms that may or may not specialize in taking companies public within a given sector, such as energy companies, mining companies, or telecommunications companies. Because the underwriters tend to specialize, the thinking is that they can place the shares at the best possible price. Brokerage houses, of course, have teams of brokers who can usually sell the shares to their best customers. While the company is shopping for a good underwriter, of course, its intention to sell shares is generally not disclosed to the public. This is considered a confidential process.

How does a company select an underwriter? In the case of a secondary offering, the company approaches firms with which it has an existing relationship, either as a market maker or provider of research. A company selling shares for the first time as an IPO relies on industry contacts to select the best firm to get the job done—namely, selling new shares at an advantageous price.

Since underwriters stand to earn a percentage of the deal, they constantly study the marketplace for companies looking to go public and then approach them in hopes of doing a deal. With millions of dollars in fees at stake, underwriters have a built-in conflict of interest when they approach a prospective company to take public. Is the move to go public really in the interest of the company? Or only in the interest of the underwriter who stands to pocket a multimillion-dollar fee? If a company agrees to do a deal simply to attract capital, it may not be in the best interests of the shareholders. The company must have a verifiable use for those funds and an ability to earn a return on the new capital. The underwriting will undoubtedly result in an increase in the number of shares outstanding, known as the float. With an increased float, a company's investors may fear dilution. This most certainly will have a negative impact on share prices.

Once a deal is struck between company and underwriter, the difficult task of writing up a prospectus gets underway. In addition, the company must file a registration form with the SEC. These forms are often boilerplate documents, and investors routinely skip over them quickly. This can be a mistake because these documents are typically all that is available on a company prior to the offering of the shares. Indeed, the SEC forbids companies from making public announcements just prior to and 25 days after trading commences in new shares. This means the information that may be critical to investor decisions is strictly limited during this period.

These rules apply so that no one party gains an edge on information concerning the status of the company. Much of what the underwriters and analysts may know at this point is considered insider information and cannot be revealed to one segment of the investment public without full disclosure to everyone. Hence, you have a lack of public information. About the only information you will see at this stage regarding a company about to be taken public is the so-called tombstone advertisements in the financial press. These ads offer very preliminary statistics regarding the underwriting—and nothing more. When a deal is in the offing, it is often in the best interest of small investors to wait until the shares are released.

The preliminary prospectus can be distributed only with what is called a red herring statement, which says the registration has not yet become effective. All this takes place in a highly regulated fashion, according to SEC guidelines. The wording of this statement must be precise and according to the regulations. This preliminary prospectus becomes the main selling tool. No research reports or other documents relating to the company can be written while the underwriting gets under way. According to SEC rules, management is not allowed to comment on any activities of the company during this time. The prospectus is the one and only document that outlines the status of the company prior to the full issuance of the shares. The reason for all these stringent regulations, of course, is to level the playing field. Small and large investors alike should all have equal access to company information. The downside is that very often little is known about the company's prospects at this time.

HOW TO READ A PROSPECTUS

The prospectus is the only reliable document containing pertinent information on the company that you are likely to find. Accordingly, as an IPO investor, you have to familiarize yourself with the format of this document and try to understand the salient points prior to purchasing shares. Here's the information it will contain:

Cover: basic information such as the name of the company and number of shares offered, including the name of the underwriter and basic regulatory statements

Prospectus Summary: short description of company

Risk Factors: may reveal potential shortfalls of company, including loss of customers, overdependence on one industry, potential legal issues, stock price volatility and liquidity

Use of Proceeds: how the company plans to use the money that is raised in the deal, whether it wants to pay down debt, finance an acquisition, or use the proceeds for general corporate purposes

Dividend Policy: most small companies won't be paying dividends

Dilution: how the issuance of the shares will have an impact on share value, including possible book value

Business: the overall view of the sector in which the company operates, including key competitors and their possible impact on the company

Management: a list of the officers and board of directors, including brief bio on each

Principal Shareholders: the big players who own the company, including funds and institutions that have large blocks of shares

Certain Transactions: list of transactions, if any, between officers and insiders and the company, including loans or leases from the company

Description of Capital Stock: number of shares, preferred stock, if any, and limited liability of directors clause

Shares Eligible for Future Sale: terms of shares held by insiders and whether and when they can sell their shares

Underwriting: how many shares the underwriters will sell and the terms of their sales agreements

Legal Matters: who the attorneys and accountants are

THE COOLING-OFF PERIOD AND ROAD SHOW

The cooling-off period extends from the date of filing the preliminary prospectus for 30 days. During this period, the SEC may comment on the impending issuance of new shares, and the underwriters are encouraged to respond by offering an amended prospectus, if necessary. If accepted, the registration becomes effective on request, and the company and underwriters are free to set up their syndicate and begin selling shares. But first there is the little matter of getting the company's story out before the investment community. This involves taking the company's story to market makers and institutional investors in what is known as a road show.

As a private investor, you are unlikely to be invited to one of these gatherings, which are typically held in major cities; their real target is the institutional investor. This organized public relations gesture is designed to inform and invite large investors to participate in the upcoming sale of the IPO. Most of the information about the company is already contained in the prospectus, so the real purpose of the road show is to create confidence in portfolio managers about management's ability to deliver on their promises. Can this management team be trusted with the institutions' money? In the days that follow, research analysts will be preparing reports—hopefully, favorable ones—and they want an opportunity to see what management has to say.

This is an important period for the IPO because the day of reckoning is rapidly approaching and the underwriters want to make sure the stock is fully subscribed when it is finally available for sale. As an individual investor, this is when you want to contact your broker and make sure he is aware of your intentions to participate in the IPO. This is a business in which having the right connections can help you, especially if all the shares are already spoken for.

A fully subscribed underwriting could result in an upward adjustment of IPO prices; a weak subscription could lead the underwriters to lower the IPO price. It all depends, as always, on supply and demand. The most widely published IPO in recent memory was that of Google. Initially sold at the seemingly high price of $85 a share, Google, within months, soared above $400 a share! So much for the supposedly high price of the IPO! Google proved to be a steal when first offered. Not every IPO can be a high-flier like Google, but IPOs do have their Wall Street versions of rock stars. What is most impressive about all of this is that yesterday's overpriced IPO becomes today's bargain-basement steal!

Behind the scenes, the final weeks before the IPO can be a period of high tension for the major players, namely, the underwriters and the institutions. Until all parties agree to the pricing of the IPO, the deal is not done. With all parties in agreement, the deal can go forward.

Be forewarned that when a hot IPO comes to market, one of several scenarios may be played out. If there is genuine competition for shares, you may not get a shot at purchasing your shares at the IPO price; IPOs have been known to surge in value within minutes of becoming public companies. If your order hasn't been filled, you then have to decide if you wish to pay up to purchase shares. By doing so, you are guaranteeing a profit to the initial lucky IPO buyer who is simply flipping shares purchased perhaps only hours earlier. Nevertheless, profits are profits—as can be readily witnessed in the free-for-all to get aboard Google.

This process of dividing up a limited number of shares among a variety of institutional players is known as final allocation. As with most profit-oriented businesses, there is the wholesale price and the retail price. The institutions, naturally, want to buy wholesale, mark up the price, and sell retail to their customers. There is no problem with paying retail—if the shares are headed higher. When it comes to participating in an IPO, it pays to have friends within the brokerage community. Understandably, most people do not have such connections. The good customers get treated better, just as the best customers in a high-end restaurant get the good tables and best service. Of course, after the shares are sold in the IPO, they take on a life of their own in the secondary market, just like any other stock. Indeed, the enthusiasm of opening day may have caused the stock to get ahead of itself, meaning there will be better buying opportunities for the stock in the days and weeks to come.

To capitalize on IPO enthusiasm, some firms are known to flip shares. But this practice is often frowned on by underwriters, who expect their participating syndicate partners to support the stock, especially in its early days. Such activities rarely go unnoticed. As a result, a firm that repeatedly flips shares won't be invited back to participate in the next IPO if they don't follow the unwritten rules. The underwriters want a successful IPO. That way, everyone makes out: the company, the underwriters, the investors. This is in sharp contrast to when a company has an IPO resulting in a one-day peak in share prices. In this instance, practically everyone is disappointed. Sure, the company may have gotten its target IPO price. But investors are typically disgruntled because they realize they overpaid. This is not the way to gather friends for long-term support of the company's shares.

The final step in the issuance of IPO shares comes when the final prospectus is printed and shipped, listing the number of shares and price on its cover. At this stage, the underwriters make the registration effective, and the stock is distributed and begins to trade. A new public company has been shepherded through inception and birth.

WHAT HAPPENS NEXT

A paradox exists when a company is about to issue a new IPO. On the one hand, analysts stop writing about the company, and management stops making public statements to the press and investors—all in compliance with the regulations concerning IPOs. On the other hand, the whisper quotient rises dramatically. Portfolio managers, especially, are apt to be talking about the stock in attempts to ascertain what is going on. Takeover specialists or like-minded companies may begin making inquiries about an impending deal. This may affect the stock's price if it is a secondary issue or, in the case of a brand-new IPO, attract potential buyers to the about-to-be-offered shares. News of the road show can cause a flurry of interest in a new stock offer. At the end of the day, however, the general trend of shares will remain a mystery. With so many countertrends likely to affect an IPO, no one can truly make an assessment before the stock begins trading.

There have been many studies performed on IPOs. Understandably, a flurry of activity is often associated with a new stock offering. Once the bloom is off the rose, however, the results are not so impressive. The message: Get there early and exit prior to any price deterioration. Studies show that following an IPO, a stock often sells *below* the offering price; in the case of secondary stock, the shareholders often use the IPO as an opportunity to sell their shares. This, of course, can also have a negative impact on prices. Ironically, despite the hoopla associated with a new IPO, the best opportunities often exist after the stock has been trading for four or five days. Those who are even more patient may see a better opportunity to purchase the stock down the road.

As an investor, you must be aware that there is a lot of money at stake in bringing an IPO to market. Management stands to gain an influx of cash, and the underwriters can earn handsome commissions. But the key question remains: Is the deal in the interest of the investor? When a brokerage company touts an IPO, you must take the information with a grain of salt. Is your broker calling you about this new opportunity because his house has instructed him to allocate the shares? If so, it may be more about the brokerage's commission in underwriting the stock than about the legitimacy of the investment. This is how Wall Street makes money.

CHAPTER 6

Insider Buying

B uying up the shares of low-priced and depressed stocks—usually selling below a dollar—has been a specialty of a friend of mine for many years now. Over that time, he has repeatedly told me he owns 9 percent of this company or that. Nine percent? Why not 7 percent or 10 percent? Why nine? The reason, of course, is quite simple. He doesn't want to be an insider, one who is required by SEC regulations to submit paperwork every time he buys or sells. By owning less than 10 percent of a company, he is no different than an investor who buys 100 shares. His investment activities are not monitored by a government agency, and he can quietly go about buying and selling as he sees fit.

Because I've been privy to some of his investment advice, I've benefited from knowing when to buy and sell. The fact is, he isn't an insider, but his finger is on the pulse of any company he chooses to make a big investment in. As a result, we've made some spectacular profits by buying early and selling when the company's story gets out before the public.

WHO IS AN INSIDER?

By definition, an *insider* is anyone who has knowledge about a company that has not yet been released to the public. Most important, insiders include company executives and directors and any shareholder who owns 10 percent or more of a company's stock. An insider could also be the printer who publishes confidential documents concerning a company that have yet to be released to the public. I once had a job working at a financial public relations firm. To write up the press releases and quarterly and annual statements, we needed to know the numbers to be published. Moreover, if a client company wanted to issue a press release, we would be the first to know. We were insiders. As a result, we were prohibited from acting on the news or telling anyone about the news prior to its release.

Can you see how having information related to an important company event can give you a significant edge? That's why acting on such information is prohibited. The investor deserves a level playing field. When ImClone's CEO told his family and Martha Stewart about the DEA's impending denial of his company's drug application before the news was released, he was violating the insider trading rule. That's why today he is in prison.

Having said this, I want to stress that there are important *legal* ways to track insider activities that can benefit the small investor. Obviously, the scandals get the publicity. But perfectly legal insider transactions take place everyday. And because of the safeguards put in place by the SEC and other regulatory agencies, the activities of these individuals can be easily tracked . . . just like footprints in the sand.

Who are the important insiders? Those people who run the company, are in control, and monitor day-to-day operations—namely, the chief executive officer (CEO) and chief financial officer (CFO). When these individuals buy and sell, it can mean something is up with the company. A member of the board of directors may buy a few hundred shares from time to time, but this is meaningless in the general scheme of things. Depending on the size of the company, there are many people who may think they understand what is going on. But despite the protestations of those CEOs and CFOs who claim they had no idea what was going on when they were caught with their hands in the cookie jar, they are typically the only ones who have a complete overview of the company. For this reason, you want to know when they buy and sell.

HOW TO TRACK THEM

Finding out what the insiders are up to is simplicity itself. The easiest way is to go to Yahoo Finance's web site and enter the symbol of the stock you are tracking. Then click Insiders under Ownership, and you will see who was buying and selling how much stock on what dates. The one drawback with this method is that there is a time lag between when the activities take place and when they are reported to the SEC.

To show you how useful this information can be, I recently went back and looked at some of the insider transactions in a stock that I owned, Input/Output (IO). On December 5, 2003, an Input/Output director by the name of James M. Lapeyre Jr. purchased a total of 2,150,000 shares at a price of $3.48. Three months later, on March 5, 2004, the price of IO had more than doubled to $7.41 a share. Mr. Lapeyre's profit was almost $8.5 million in three months! See Figure 6.1.

In another insider transaction, Input/Output's CEO, Robert P. Peebler, purchased a more modest 25,800 shares on May 3, 2005, between $5.85 and $5.95 per share. Six months later, on November 3, 2005, IO shares closed at $8.45 a share. See Figure 6.2.

I want to stress that these were perfectly legal, fully disclosed transactions. But the inference to be drawn is clear. Insiders have a pretty good idea when their companies' fortunes are about to change for the better or the worse. In these two examples, one clue was the size of the transaction; the other clue was who was making the transaction. I selected Input/Output because I was familiar with the company and owned the stock. But there are many, many more examples of intelligent insider buying that you can find by simply noting when the purchases were made and tracking the progress of the stock.

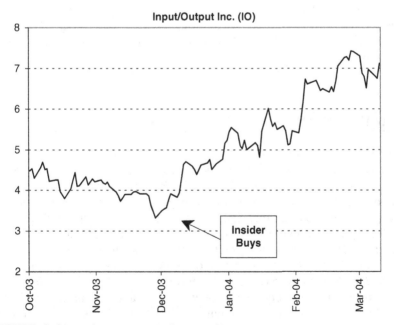

FIGURE 6.1 Insider Transaction for Input/Output

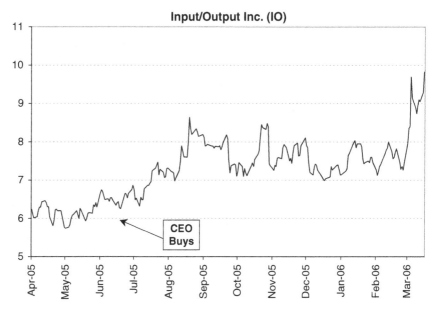

FIGURE 6.2 Another Input/Output Insider Transaction

The SEC does its own compilation of insider transactions and publishes the information in its monthly *Official Summary of Security Transactions and Holdings*. The drawback is that the information is dated and sells for $111 a year.

SMALL STOCKS HAVE THE EDGE

To the investor in small stocks, the insider transactions provide an edge not available to large-cap investors, according to two professors who have studied the insider transaction data. Professors Josef Lakonishok and Inmoo Lee, of the University of Illinois and Case Western Reserve University, respectively, maintain that insider transactions are useless indicators for selecting well-known stocks. Unless the companies are under $300 million in capitalization, these data don't correlate, according to their studies.

A similar observation was made by Mark Hulbert in an article published in *Forbes* some years ago. His newsletter, *Hulbert Financial Digest*, which monitors the success of newsletter writers, reported that insider trading was a poor stock-selection tool. Yet, Hulbert was concentrating on large-cap companies, those with capitalization in excess of $1 billion.

The stock prices of smaller companies, however, tended to respond much more readily to insider transactions. The reasons for this were twofold:

1. Smaller companies were more likely to be in a turnaround phase, and insider buying tended to reflect the changing fortunes of the smaller companies.
2. Smaller companies were apt to have fewer shares outstanding, suggesting that even a modest increase in buying could enhance share values.

In the case of insider buying versus selling, it seems that the primary focus of buying was quite simple: The buyers thought the stock was about to trade higher. Selling, however, might take place for a variety of reasons, ranging from personal reasons to tax considerations.

The size of the insider transactions, as illustrated in the Input/Output example, tends to indicate that serious buying is done when the insider has a serious point of view about the stock's prospects. In the case of small purchases, chances are a director might pick up a few hundred or few thousand shares just to be seen as part of the team. But insiders who want to make serious money on what they see as a strong long-term trend cannot hide their activities, given the SEC guidelines. Thus, their footprints are available for all to see.

In looking through the transactions records, you will note that not every insider transaction is accomplished in the open market. Some involve exercising options; others involve selling shares that were given to individuals for whatever reason, perhaps as a term in their employment contract. Pay special attention to the market purchases. When insiders put their own money on the line, chances are they see a very real opportunity. When insiders have been granted options, their personal stake is obviously not as great as when they make an outright purchase.

Pay attention to the quality of the insider buying. The buying activities of a chief financial officer who buys even a modest amount of stock with his own money might be more significant than a wealthy director who buys a lot more. The money may be more meaningful to the chief financial officer, suggesting the impending move in the stock is more likely.

Also look for a number of insiders to do the same thing. If three or four company insiders start buying the stock, it is probably more significant than if one officer buys. If you have both buying and selling during the same period, however, you may want to hold off on buying because the messages are mixed.

As a rule, you want to stay away from companies in which the insiders own too little or too much of the stock. In the first instance, why would management not want a stake in the company? Too little ownership suggests management is more interested in taking from the company instead of putting value in. Too much ownership means the outside shareholders are at the whims of management and holding an illiquid stock. For this reason, look for insider ownership to be between 10 and 30 percent.

Ironically, the most potent use of insider information is as a contrary indicator. This is likely to occur when merger talks are underway and management refuses to talk about the terms of an impending deal. Indeed, the company may even issue a written denial of any discussions concerning a buyout or takeover because management doesn't want to muddy the waters prior to an announcement. But the investor who can read between the lines might be able to see a hidden yes amid the repeated denials. Companies that are said to be not for sale often go on the auction block. So if the CEO isn't talking—or is protesting that the company isn't for sale too loudly—the investor may want to take that as a sign that the very opposite will occur—and buy shares in anticipation of a takeover or buyout. Needless to say, such occurrences often reap windfall profits for astute investors who acted before the announcement.

CHAPTER 7

The Selection Process

The day of reckoning has finally arrived. You've scraped together $25,000 to $40,000, opened your brokerage account, and acquired a sophisticated software charting program. Now you want to make some serious money. You've opened your financial newspaper to the stock pages. But the sheer number of stocks leaves you feeling bewildered. Where do you begin?

Let's assume you've decided to find some hidden gem languishing at a support level. It is now time to begin scrolling through some price charts. It won't be long before you will recognize a beaten-down highflier such as a Sun Microsystems or a JDSU getting ready to regain its glory. Even a Lucent Technologies, long since beaten down out of the stratosphere, may appeal to you on a technical basis. But let's say you want to move beyond technical considerations. How do you find a truly undervalued stock?

ASSET PLAYS AND CONCEPT STOCKS

To find value, you have to consider the realm of fundamental analysis, the murky area where even fundamentalists cannot agree on what constitutes value. There are so many approaches to determining value in the market that practically no one can agree on the best one. For one, there are those who swear by so-called asset plays. An asset play is typically a mine with the asset still in ground. Will the company be able to extract the value out of the mine? Will the costs of extracting the metal or mineral exceed the value of the final product? Does the asset really exist? I once owned shares in an oil company that had leases and little else. Inept at getting to the oil in the ground, the company spent thousands of dollars on experts, which prompted one investor to quip, "The oil would have been cheaper if they had driven around to gas stations and purchased it at the pump." They later went broke.

On the other hand, when you have a stock like First Quantum or Northern Orion, the mined assets create a bonanza of riches for the fortunate investors. In recent years, asset play companies that own real estate, oil and mineral rights, and patents on emerging technologies have all had their day in the sun. Like everything in life, some asset plays work, and some don't.

Investors like companies that make money. A company can have all the assets in the world, but unless they can capitalize on those assets, they offer only a promise. For a stock to make a significant rise, it must have results.

When it comes to concept stocks, a similar rule applies; namely, you must have results. A concept stock is based on an idea, a new theory, perhaps a dream—something that has not yet been brought to market but, according to its proponents, very well could be. Also known as story stocks, concept stocks could be anything. This is not to say that concept stocks are all pie in the sky. Fifteen years ago, the notion of a company profiting from the Internet—AOL, Google, Oracle—was a concept. These companies were story stocks. And 30 years ago, companies that have become mainstays in the personal computer business, such as Dell, would have been concept stocks. See Figure 7.1 for an example of a concept stock going mainstream.

Many concept stocks fail not because the idea is faulty, but because the company runs out of capital, doesn't know how to market the product, or simply has poor management. One rule to steer you away from concept stocks is an abundance of hype. If a new concept is being hyped as the newest great thing and a can't-fail investment, be cautious. Chances are, the IPO funds will be going into the pockets of the promoters, and the investors are going to be left holding the bag. Practically every week, I receive a glossy brochure in my mail telling me of the potential for a fabulous new stock that is going to be the next Wal-Mart or Microsoft. When you read the fine print, however, you find out that the newsletter writer has been given a large fee to promote the shares. Any such promotional piece should be seen strictly for what it is—a promotional piece. A company with a legitimate new concept will, in time, find its audience without the hyping from fake newsletter writers.

Without sounding biased against certain stock exchanges, I should note that you want to be wary of low-priced so-called Bulletin Board stocks, as well as stocks trading on the Vancouver Exchange, which is often a hotbed of concept stocks. I like Canadian stocks and have done quite well investing in them, but you are typically better off buying a stock

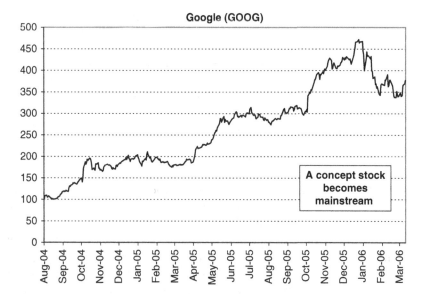

Google (GOOG)

A concept stock becomes mainstream

FIGURE 7.1 Google Goes from Concept Stock to Mainstream

on the Toronto Stock Exchange, Canada's leading exchange, than some of the highfliers in Vancouver.

A stock is probably a better investment candidate if it is traded in Toronto as opposed to Vancouver or on the NASDAQ as opposed to the Bulletin Board sheets. As you go up the ladder to the New York Stock Exchange, there are increasingly stringent listing requirements.

GUIDELINES

As a rule, you want to find hidden value or value that has, for a variety of reasons, been overlooked when you are considering a good stock to buy. This is not always easy because a lot of talented people are out there beating the bushes for just such a bargain. Nevertheless, let us list a few of the guidelines:

1. **Profitability.** This is tough one because a highly profitable company will already have a stock price that reflects that profitability. Better to look for a company on the verge of profitability, one perhaps still in a loss situation, which, significantly, is losing less money month to month or quarter to quarter. The difficulty with selecting a company based on profitability alone is that you have no idea whether the

company is going to be able to sustain those profits. What will happen if you buy the stock of a company that is consistently profitable? The risk is that the company may have grown complacent and the profits may not be there in the future—meaning the stock is going to take a dive. An unprofitable company, on the other hand, may be doing all the right things to ensure future profitability. In this instance, you will have a low-priced or underpriced stock primed to run higher. If you have a track record of underperformance, however, you want an explanation why the future should be better. A change in the management team, with a new proven moneymaker at the helm, might be all you need to create a turnaround. Likewise, if a savvy management has been investing in a company's future, today's stock price may not reflect the potential already in place. When the profits begin to hit the bottom line, the price of the shares will most certainly move up.

2. **Capitalization.** The smaller the number of shares available (usually under 100 million), the better. There are exceptions to this. Consider Sirius Satellite Radio with 1.33 billion shares outstanding. In the past year, the stock has risen almost 68 percent. This stock has moved higher despite the size of the float. The fewer the number of shares, the less buying is required to overwhelm selling and drive up the price of the stock. Supply and demand will always be the arbiter of higher prices. With fewer shares (less supply), a company that attracts new buyers (new demand) is likely to see higher prices as a result.

3. **Future.** What does the future hold for this company? Is it in a growing field or a stagnant one? Does it have a specialty patent that will enable it to stay out in front? What about the competition? Can someone else deliver the same product cheaper? Investing is all about the future, so that's where your focus should be.

4. **Market makers.** The more the merrier. Many people making a market in the stock—meaning they are willing to buy when you sell, and vice versa—is a good sign for a stock for two reasons: One, it signifies interest in the stock; two, the so-called spread between the bid and the asked will be small. This means you have to give up less when you buy and sell. By contrast, a thinly traded stock is often illiquid. To draw out a buyer or seller to take the other side of the trade, you are required to give up more because the spread—the difference between bid and asked price—is wider.

5. **Recent price activity.** If a stock is on the radar screen of would-be investors, the stock price reflects that activity. Very often, a stock moves in anticipation of impending news. You only have to consult the daily volume statistics and compare them with the average volume to see whether a stock is enjoying enhanced activity.

NUTS AND BOLTS

Traditionalists ask a very simple question when they are trying to identify a star performer among the thousands of stocks available to investors: What's the company worth? By taking the stock's current price and multiplying by the number of shares outstanding, the current value is readily determined. But the burning question is not what value the market places on the stock today, but, quite simply, what will the price be tomorrow—in 6 months, 9 months, a year, 2 years? Understandably, if the valuation is going to be considerably higher, you have a potential winner on your hands.

One approach is to look at a company's balance sheet and subtract liabilities from current assets. You might be considered wealthy if you have $3 million in the bank. But would you feel the same way if you owed $10 million? Of course, you wouldn't. That's why this simple measurement of a company's worth, known as book value, is so important. You might make the case that in an ideal world, a company would trade exactly at book value. But as you will see, this is far from the truth. A good company can trade far in excess of book value and still be a good investment. That's because investors are always looking to the future and view the stock in terms of its future revenues and earnings. Hence, the book value might be just $9 a share, but the stock may be trading at $20 or even $25. The opposite is also true. A good stock again may be trading below book value, in which case, it may be a good investment. An overvalued stock, of course, may also trade above or below book value. Because we live in an imperfect world, many factors determine a stock's market price, the book value being just one of them.

Fundamental analysts have devised a series of measurements in an attempt to quantify stock choices. Whereas the book value is considered the real value of the company, the price the stock market places on the company could, perhaps, be called the unreal number. But you'll never find a stockbroker willing to sell a stock at the book value. The only price you will ever get is what the market agrees is the current price—the market price.

Accordingly, when we divide the book value price into the aggregate value of all the available stock, we have what is called the price-to-book ratio. Again, this is a number that analysts like to throw around. The rule: A high price-to-book ratio suggests the stock is expensively priced; a low price-to-book suggests a bargain.

This type of analysis would be simple if it weren't for a number of other pesky problems that plague fundamentalists. What about the value of so-called good will or intellectual property or brand names? A bricks-and-mortar company might lend itself to a thorough appraisal, but what about a concept company like Amazon.com, whose value stems from its ability to sell over the Internet? Does its book value really tell the whole story?

Clearly, using a price-to-book ratio to value assets is subject to a number of vagaries. A company with considerable tangible assets may carry its building at little or no cost, and a company with nonsalable assets, which have no value outside its narrow area of expertise, may overvalue an asset that, in truth, has no real market value.

Before you throw up your hands in frustration, rest assured that the price-to-book ratio is simply one benchmark that analysts use and that, in general, it is widely accepted as a fairly reasonable estimate of value. There was a time, however, not too long ago, during the Internet bubble, when traditional measurements such as this one no longer worked since the market was truly out of line. This has since not been the case. Stock prices have come back to earth. And as a general rule, stocks are now occasionally selling below book, meaning there are opportunities out there.

Over the years, a number of studies have illustrated the wisdom of buying stocks selling below net asset value, that is, below book. One of the fathers of fundamental analysis, Benjamin Graham, recommended that investors buy only stocks selling at 65 percent or less of underlying net asset value. Putting Graham's assertion to the test, a professor looked at the behavior of stocks for the 13-year period between 1970 and 1983. What if, asked the study, you only purchased stocks selling below 65 percent of net asset value and held them for one year? Would you make money, and if so, how would you compare with the studies of the overall market? Moreover, what if you then moved on to other stocks filling this criterion? Concentrating solely on stocks trading on the New York and American Stock Exchanges, the study definitely showed that you would earn an astonishing 29 percent as compared with just 12 percent for stocks overall. Perhaps there is something to be said for this low price-to-value buying strategy.

In a similar 17-year study, the percentages favored the low book value by 14 percent to 6 percent. Another research team, using slightly different but similar criteria over a 20-year period, showed that a low price-to-book value was the deciding factor is selecting stocks. The lowest valuation stocks gained a whopping 41 percent versus just a 1 percent gain in the highest valuation stocks. The moral: Buy low-priced stocks selling at low price-to-book values!

The same pattern was found in international stocks. If you can find a stock selling cheaply compared to its net asset value, buy it!

You could make the case that these data are skewed because, in the case of a bull market, a rising tide lifts all boats. In a bull market, you could sometimes simply throw a dart, buy whatever stock it lands on, and make money. Fair enough. But what about down years when the selection criteria become far more important? The investors who purchased any stocks near the March 2000 market tops were severely punished for throwing the notion of asset valuation out the window. I remember Lucent Technologies selling in the mid-80s back then. Today it is having trouble getting over $3 a share.

Over time, we are told, the stock market will outperform virtually any other investment—bonds and real estate being its primary competitor for investment dollars. But do you really think investors who paid $80 a share for Lucent five or six years ago will ever see that price again in their lifetimes? Chances are it won't happen. The moral: Be careful when you ignore net asset value in a stock you are thinking of buying.

MONEY MANAGEMENT

There are different schools of thought when it comes to deciding not just what to buy, but how you buy. Assume for a moment that you have already found your low-priced and undervalued stock. Do you place all your bets on the table at once? Or do you hold off for a while, perhaps waiting to see how the investment does? One approach is that a good value is a good value. Load the boat while you can. Place all your bets before the stock begins to run. Another question: What if you are indeed correct? Do you take profits at the same time? Let's put the selling aside for a moment. The load-the-boat strategy has its pros and cons. If you are right, you will probably be congratulating yourself for the wisdom of your decision. The other side of the coin, however, suggests you may have been a bit premature. Do you buy more? By definition, if you have already spent all your investment funds, you are no longer in a position to buy more. If you buy at different levels, a strategy known as dollar cost averaging (buying more as the stock moves lower), you will have an overall lower entry price. Should your shares subsequently go higher, of course, the payoff will be even more impressive than the winning results of the plunger. Yet, here again, there is a downside. What if you add to your position and the stock continues lower? You will still have a loss.

It helps to have a plan of action before you find yourself forced to make a decision. Like so many rules, of course, this one is easier said than done. A conservative approach, utilized by many seasoned Wall Streeters, is to remove some of your profits on the first run up—assuming, of course, that there is one. Known as getting your bait off the table, this strategy calls for taking profits on half your position once the stock doubles in value from your entry price. In a low-priced stock, doubling is no big thing. It happens all the time. But consider the wisdom of this approach. Let's say you purchase XYZ stock for $1.50 a share. Commissions aside, you invested $15,000 and bought a total of 10,000 shares. The stock now rises to $3 and you sell half your position, or 5,000 shares. There's your $15,000 bait money. The other 5,000 shares are now free to trade higher or lower. Regardless of what happens, you won't be taking a loss.

This is a conservative strategy because the woulda, coulda, shoulda crowd will be gloating and calling you a shortsighted chicken if the stock subsequently rises to, let's say, $5 a share. Now your $3.50 profit on 10,000 shares ($35,000) will net you only half that amount, or $17,500, because you sold half your position on the first double to $3. Should the stock subsequently sell down, however, it will be your turn to gloat. This may put you on the horns of a dilemma, but there are, as you can see, worse places to be.

At the end of the day, how you manage your money is probably second in importance only to stock selection. We are forever reading in the newspapers about some low-income individual who died and left a fortune to a trusted friend or charitable organization. Everyone, naturally, is surprised, because the person in question never displayed any signs of wealth; on the contrary, the person typically was very frugal. How do they do it? By utilizing sound money-management techniques, coupled with the power of compounding or reinvesting profits. Even a small amount of money that is repeatedly doubled grows at a rapid pace.

REVENUES AND EARNINGS

Nothing is more confusing to the new investor than the relationship of revenues and earnings, or income. Revenues are the amounts of money that a company takes in; earnings are what it gets to keep. As a former employee of a financial public relations firm, I can tell you that putting the proper spin on a company's quarterly and annual results was always prominent in our minds lest we alienate our clients. No matter how dismal the results, the company executives always wanted the financial reports issued to shareholders to appear in the best possible light. Accordingly, if revenues were up, we would highlight this fact, even if a ton of expenses in the previous quarter caused the company to lose money. This also meant emphasizing the positive, always looking ahead to the results in the next quarter. A typical quarterly shareholder letter might appear as follows:

Dear Shareholders:

As CEO of XYZ Plastic Piping, I am pleased to report that we have finally turned the corner in the delivery of our new and revolutionary plastic piping system. In the fiscal quarter ending on March 31, 2006,

XYZ generated record revenues of $4.3 million as compared to revenues of $3.5 million during the same period last year. Due to a one-time cost related to the reengineering of our piping system, however, earnings fell during the same period to $427,000 ($.07 per share) as compared to earnings of $567,000 ($.09 per share) during the same period last year.

We here at XYZ Plastic Piping are fully confident we are headed in the right direction and that we will indeed reach—and possibility exceed—our corporate goals as set forth in last year's annual report. During the first quarter, we were fortunate to bring on board a new vice president in charge of corporate finance and make other changes necessary to become more competitive in the weeks and months ahead. Thank you for your continuing support!

J.D. Jones
CEO

As you can see from this letter, earnings were actually down. The company is worse off in terms of income than it was a year ago. Nevertheless, the company is touting record revenues. The problem is that the money isn't getting to the bottom line. Having owned stocks in companies that often report record revenues, I can tell you that if the revenues don't make it to the bottom line, the stock is likely to do poorly. Investors want earnings, not revenues. While enhanced revenues often accompany larger earnings, the trick is getting to keep the money in the company coffers.

There are dozens of reasons why higher revenues often don't translate into higher earnings—some legitimate and some less so. When you read the small print in the financial disclosure statements, you may find that management has granted itself a pay raise or that the company expenses have suddenly soared because of some unforeseen event. As a rule, companies try to keep too much money from going to the bottom line lest they have to pay federal income taxes on the profits. But there are a million ways to spend money and otherwise fritter away shareholder equity. Without being a trained certified public accountant, you may have trouble recognizing mismanagement of company funds. Nevertheless, a company that has difficulty getting the money to the bottom line may not prove to be a good investment candidate.

CASH FLOW

In recent years, amid a boatload of scandals, the emphasis on the bottom line has caused some companies to get themselves in deep water. We all know the headline-grabbing stories, but what about those companies, while not exactly fraudulent, that fudge the numbers? Understandably, this has been a cause for concern in the investment community, and not a few investors today are taking a skeptical look at earnings reports. Can these numbers be trusted? To deal with this new skepticism, some analysts are taking new measures to evaluate a company's earnings.

A corporate income statement starts with total revenues and then subtracts expenses to arrive at earnings. The expenses could be anything: rent, wages, interest on company debt, the cost of artwork adorning the CEO's office, depreciation of equipment. Because a company can throw anything into the expense pile, including the cost of the corporate sink, you must be especially rigorous in attempting to ascertain which expenses are legitimate and which ones aren't.

The rule is to be wary of expenses hidden deep in a financial statement, such as the loan to a CEO to purchase his second home in the mountains of Montana. To get past the nonessentials, therefore, you want to concentrate on cash flow, or what's left over from revenues after you deduct the cost of generating those revenues. This is also known as the price-to-cash flow ratio. Ever hear of EBITDA? This means earnings before interest, taxes, depreciation, and amortization. Practically every CPA uses this number to characterize a clear view of how well a company is doing.

Cash flow frequently provides a clearer view of company operations in terms of the real bottom line.

The price-to-cash flow ratio is determined by dividing the money a company generates by the market capitalization. A low ratio suggests we are getting plenty of bang for our investment buck; a high ratio suggests the opposite, meaning the stock is probably overpriced. In studies ranging over a 20-year period, companies with low price-to-cash flow ratios performed the best.

PRICE-TO-SALES

Here's another benchmark that is easy to calculate. Take the company's revenues and divide it by the total market capitalization. Another way is to divide the price of a share of stock by the annual sales per share. You should get the same number. At least with sales, we know something is coming in the door. This ratio will tell you if the stock is cheap; a low price-to-sales number is indicative of a company that is able to generate sales at low cost. A high ratio, on the other hand, suggests the company is spending too much per dollar of sales and needs to tighten up its spending habits or find a more lucrative line of business. The bottom line, of course, is ultimately profits—not sales. Even if the cost of sales is low, the key question remains: Can the company get the money to the bottom line?

An example of this cost of doing business analysis was recently highlighted in the press. With oil prices up, gas stations were experiencing increasing problems with drive-away customers—people who pumped gasoline and then left without paying. It turns out the gas station owner is only banking pennies on the $3.00 per gallon price. With drive-aways increasing, a single missed sale can jeopardize the owner's daily profit. Clearly, there was no windfall for the gas station owners in the recent run-up in oil prices.

As you can see, revenue is a difficult barometer of a company's future success. You can have impressive revenues with no profits; on the other hand, you can have modest revenues and encouraging profits. In highly competitive businesses, pennies count. But in industries with more generous margins, there is more room for error. This is why the airline industry is usually a tough business to make money in. With the mix of unstable fuel prices and enormous labor costs, there is rarely anything left at the end of the day—hence the rash of airline bankruptcies. A biotech startup, however, with a fascinating new FDA-approved drug, could bank 20 or 30 cents on every dollar of sales.

The price-to-sales ratio has gained a number of supporters among analysts in recent years because so many companies have had no earnings, making the age-old P/E ratio archaic. What about earnings? In the new age of the Internet, earnings became perhaps viable down the road. But, in the meantime, the shares rose on promise and little else. With untenable price/earnings ratios, the analysts sought refuge in price-to-sales metrics. But because so many firms were plowing through their new IPO money at increasing rates, even these ratios were marginal at best. These new high-fliers were pursuing market share at all costs in hopes of earnings, one day, finding their way to the bottom line. Ultimately, the valuations were unsustainable and the market crashed.

BALANCE SHEET BASICS

Unless you are a CPA, chances are your eyes grow bleary when it comes to a company's financials—primarily the income statement and the balance sheet. These statements are drawn up by professional accountants in accordance with specific industry standards—standards that, naturally, are primarily understood by others in the accounting profession. Despite a few bad apples in the accounting profession who misrepresented companies' earnings in recent years, the bulk of all accounting is performed at a very high level. Moreover, because the accountants are independent of the companies they work for, they do a good job in reporting a company's finances lest they be called on the carpet—and held liable—in a scandal resulting from a fudging of the numbers in a professional audit.

What does the average nonaccountant need to know about corporate accounting? Namely, that there are pitfalls to be avoided in sizing up a company. Even a cursory reading of a company's annual or quarterly report, however, can provide an important clue as to the company's future prospects.

First, let's consider the balance sheet. The left side of the balance sheet lists assets. On the right side, the balance sheet lists the liabilities of the business, which have a first claim on assets. The sources of ownership (equity) capital in the business are presented below the liabilities, to emphasize that the liabilities have the higher or prior claim on the assets. Put another way, this means that the creditors and bondholders will be paid first, should there be any claim against assets. The shareholders get only what's left after the creditors have been satisfied. In a worst-case scenario—namely, bankruptcy—this means nothing.

In reading a balance sheet, nonaccountants can skip down to major categories. Total current assets is the subtotal of all the individual assets. Even more important categories, and the final entry, are highlighted by a double line, such as total assets.

The balance sheet is prepared at the close of business for a given time period. Hence, an income statement for the period ending on June 30, 2006, lists the income for that quarter or fiscal year. It is as if time is frozen on that date. Income coming in on the following day would then be entered into the period for the next quarter or fiscal year. You need to understand that the balance sheet reports only the final single number, not the flow of money in and out of a company. For example, a company may report assets of $7.4 million at the close of one reporting period. But if, for example, it had to pay out $2.4 million for a loan payment the following day (after the fiscal period is over), the assets would fall to $5.0 million a day later. The balance sheet, therefore, is a snapshot of a company's worth at a given moment in time.

Be mindful that the balance sheet numbers are not listed haphazardly. The specific format is as follows:

Left Side	**Right Side**
Current assets	Current liabilities
Long-term operating assets	Long-term liabilities
Other assets	Owners' equity

Current assets are cash and other assets that will be converted into cash during one operating cycle. The operating cycle refers to the basic rhythm of the company. This is when it manufactures products or provides services and generates the income from those products or services. Long-term operating assets are not held for sale to customers; rather, they are used on a daily basis to operate the business. These can be either tangible or nontangible assets. The former could be buildings or factories; the latter are apt to be patents or copyrights that play an important role in generating income for the company. Tangible assets are also known as fixed assets. Land is the more likely fixed asset, but this term also applies to equipment and machinery, trucks, forklifts, furniture, telephones, computers, and so on.

Current liabilities are those that depend on the conversion of current assets into cash for their payment. These usually require payment within one year. Long-term liabilities require payment more than a year after the balance sheet date. In general, liabilities are demands for payment from current assets.

Ironically, an increased liability can also cause a company's assets to rise. This would occur when a company borrows money. Yes, the company now must pay back the loan; but it has also increased the value of its assets on hand by borrowing the funds. Should a company buy goods to manufacture a product on credit, its liabilities will rise, but so also will its inventories. As with any loan that has not yet been paid back, when the company borrows, it increases its total assets. Consider the case of an individual who takes out a mortgage to purchase a home. The value of the home may increase during the time he holds the mortgage. While the mortgage must be paid back, the enhanced value of the home is the homeowner's to keep, should he sell the house. The same is true for a corporation.

An important concept to understand when you look at a balance sheet is book value. The original cost of a company's assets may decline as time goes on. The book value, therefore, must not be confused with current replacement value. Should equipment have to be replaced, the book value number would often be quite inadequate. In that case, the company would have to undertake enhanced liability in paying current replacement costs for today's new equipment.

When a company, therefore, writes off equipment, by taking a tax deduction or depreciation allowance, on its tax returns, it attempts to write off only the original cost of the equipment—not the replacement cost. The bottom line is that, should the equipment ultimately need replacing, the company will probably incur a one-time cost that will negatively impact its earnings.

The basic accounting rule is that fixed assets should be depreciated over the life of the asset, not on a one-time basis during the year the asset is acquired. The book value of assets, therefore, is the original cost minus the depreciation. The purpose of writing off the value of fixed assets is to provide a true and accurate accounting of cash flow. With the possible exception of land and real estate, fixed assets tend to lose value over time. In trying to ascertain the value of a company, therefore, you have to take into account whether its holdings fall into this category of depreciating assets. If they do, the company may be faced with the expenses of replacing them in the near future.

As you can see, there are many imponderables when it comes to trying to figure out what a company is really worth. Some companies, such as airlines, have high fixed-asset expenses. Others, such as a software company that specializes in creating video games, might have very low costs associated with running its business. It can lease offices and computers and offer its employees a piece of the business, in the form of stock options, in return for low salaries. Can you see how the former might have a harder time generating the kind of profits that would cause the stock to soar? A company that has high fixed expenses must perform month after month just to meet its current obligations. A small software company, on the other hand, may have modest start-up costs and generate impressive profits right out of the gate with the right product. It was the hopes of the latter example that caused stock values to take off during the late nineties' Internet boom.

UNDERSTANDING RETURN ON INVESTMENT (ROI)

The two types of financial statements, the balance sheet and the profit-and-loss statement, are at the heart of a sound fundamental analysis of any given company. But you must understand how to move beyond these two benchmark measurements to really understand how the company is doing. The easiest way to interpret a company's results is by looking at the key ratios accepted in the financial community.

The rate of return (ROI) is among the most important of these ratios. This is calculated by taking the profit and dividing it by the investment. Yet this brings up a key question: What, exactly, is profit? Net operating profit, profit after taxes, profit before taxes—all could be profit. The same ambiguity applies to the word *investment*. Are we talking about total assets employed or merely equity? It makes a difference. It is important that a company makes the definitions of these terms clear and that it is consistent in reporting the numbers.

For the sake of this illustration, let's use profit after taxes and total assets. Let's assume we are looking at a company we'll call ABC Technologies. Here's the simple calculation to determine ROI:

$$\frac{\text{Net profit}}{\text{Total assets}} = \frac{\$37,000}{\$279,000} = .132, \text{ or } 13.2\%$$

According to these results, ABC Technologies is earning a rate of return of 13.2 percent on its invested capital.

Now, as an investor, you might be comparing ABC with two other investment opportunities. One is a semiconductor company with an ROI of 25.1 percent, and the other is a financial services company with an ROI of 7.9 percent. Based on the sole criteria of ROI, the semiconductor company would win hands down because it is utilizing its invested capital in the most effective way possible.

This is the key to understanding this ratio: How much money can the company make per invested dollar? Put another way, what investment will give me the most bang for the buck? You should note the following: A company's net profit on sales may be high, but if the sales volume is low for the capital invested, the rate of return on the investment may be low. This highlights why rate of return is important as compared to simply looking at sales volume, profit on sales, and absolute profit figures. A company that can do more with less is almost always a better investment opportunity than one that requires substantial capital outlays to generate healthy sales.

The rate of return on investment is nothing more than an investment tool for measuring a company's performance. Its drawback, as with any ratio, is that it measures what has already taken place, not what lies ahead. The idea is to compare the ratio with competing companies. The ROI ratio can also provide you with a glimpse into the trend of a given company. Is it maintaining its ROI, or is the company making less money on the same investment? In the latter case, you may have an argument for selling the stock if you already own it.

DEBT

There are two schools of thought on investing in a company that has debt, both of them with merit. You could make the argument that a debt-free company is preferable to one that has debt. A company without debt is unlikely to be pushed into bankruptcy. That is a big plus for investors. But the general rules for undertaking debt that apply to consumers likewise apply in the corporate world. So-called good debt is when you invest in an appreciating asset, such as a home mortgage, a postgraduate education, or a business start-up. Few people would argue with the wisdom of taking on debt for these items. Bad debt, on the other hand, is when you use the borrowed funds to finance a depreciating asset, such as an automobile, a holiday in the Caribbean, or expensive jewelry. The bottom line: Will the asset be worth more in the future? When it comes to corporate debt, the same guidelines should be observed. Yet, since almost all profit-making enterprises have the same corporate goal—to earn a profit—the use of those funds to generate revenues and profits down the road must be uppermost in management's mind.

Taking our analogy a step further, who hasn't witnessed the aggressive marketing techniques of the credit card industry? If you are a teenager or even the family dog, some credit card company has probably gotten your name and tried to solicit you into signing up for its low interest rates. The result has been an unprecedented rise in bankruptcies. When it comes to companies, especially during boom times, the lure of easy money may become too much to resist. The biggest investment mistake I ever made was to purchase shares in a small cellular phone company that had almost a billion dollars in debt, presumably to expand their wireless communications. Given the burgeoning competition in the telecommunications business, the company was unable to grow fast enough to pay off the loan. The bottom line was Chapter 11 and a wiping out of all the shareholders' equity.

On the other hand, responsible debt can be exactly what the doctor ordered. A company that can successfully utilize borrowed funds can grow more rapidly than a conservative company that doesn't use other people's money to ramp up operations. When it comes to analyzing a company's debt, perhaps the best way is the middle way: Too much debt can spell disaster, but too little debt suggests slow growth. The key is management's ability to use the debt effectively. It comes down to trust in management.

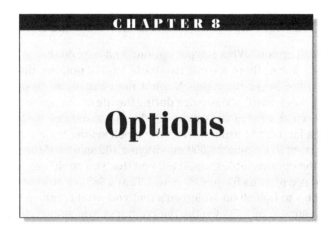

CHAPTER 8

Options

O ptions can be a useful tool for investors looking to maximize their gains. For the individual who is focusing on low-priced stocks, they can be especially beneficial because they allow the buyer to control an asset worth many times the cost of the initial investment. They are normally bought and sold on listed options exchanges and cover virtually all the household-name stocks.

To give you an idea of the value of options, consider the difference in the cost of purchasing a stock versus buying the option. With Dow Chemical recently trading just under $42 a share, a 100-share purchase would cost approximately $4,200. Yet a call option on Dow shares for the next 30 days would cost just 30 cents a share, or $30 for the 100 shares. Incredibly, the call option would provide its buyer the same profit above the so-called strike price as someone who bought the shares would make.

Options provide what is known as leverage. Put in simple terms, this means you get more bang for the buck. And that's why they are so popular with investors. With our Dow Chemical example, the same $4,200 that would be required to purchase 100 shares could be used to buy 140 call options. That means the buyer of the options would control the equivalent of 14,000 shares of Dow as opposed to just 100 shares. Every $1 move above the call's strike price would make a whopping $14,000 for the buyer of the calls.

While this is an extreme example, it does illustrate the potential for profitability in buying options.

THE BASICS

What is a call option? What is a put option? And how do they work? As you may already know, there are just two basic kind of options: puts and calls. Calls allow the buyer the right—but not the obligation—to purchase the underlying stock at the strike price during the life of the option. So let's say you are down at your local Walgreens Pharmacy and you notice that they are doing a landslide business. With the stock selling for $43 a share, you might not want to commit $4,300 into buying 100 shares of the stock. But a glance at the options tables would tell you that you could buy a call option good for three months for just 85 cents. That's $85 for 100 shares. Indeed, you might be so bullish on Walgreen's that you would pick up ten calls for a total investment of $850. On the ten contracts, you stand to make $1,000 on every point, or dollar, the stock gains above the strike price.

The beauty of options is their flexibility. If you think a stock is overvalued and due for a fall, you simply buy put options as opposed to calls. A put gives you the right, during the life of the option, to sell the underlying stock at the strike price. So if you think Walgreens Pharmacy shares are due for a break, you simply buy puts. Should the stock decline, you can either exercise the option or simply sell the option in the options market. Your profit will be the difference between the strike price and the market price of the stock at the time you sell the option. For example, with Walgreens trading at $42 a share, you buy a put with a 40 strike good for three months. Should the price fall to 35, you earn the difference between 40 (the strike price) and 35 (the market price of the stock). The difference is yours to keep.

What if your judgment proves faulty and the stock doesn't move? As an option buyer, you stand to lose your investment. But you can never lose more than the cost of the option. The bottom line: You have a fixed cost but an unlimited potential.

THE TERMS OF AN OPTION

Every option investor must understand the basic terms of an option and how they differ from a simple stock purchase. When you purchase a stock, you pay the full amount (unless you purchase the stock on margin), and you then gain ownership of the stock. This is comparable to buying a house or automobile for cash. You make the investment, and the underlying asset is yours.

When you buy a call or put option, however, you simply buy the right to purchase or sell the shares of the underlying asset at a fixed price at some time in the future. This is an important point, because an option is what is known as a wasting asset. At expiration, the option will either have value or no value. If it has value, the buyer is entitled to take the profit or whatever the option will bring. If the option is said to be out of the money, however, the option will have no value, and the entire premium cost, or the cost of the option, will be lost.

Let's see how this might work in practice. Let's say you are a long-term bull on Wal-Mart shares. With Wal-Mart trading at $45 a share, you decide to buy a Wal-Mart March 45 call trading for $1.60. Your total expense on the call is just $160 for 100 shares. March refers to the expiration month of the option, and 45 refers to the strike price, the price at which you can exercise the call. Now you know that if Wal-Mart shares rise above 45 in the time left until the expiration of the call, you can profit at the rate of $100 per call per dollar rise in the underlying stock. If, for example, by expiration, Wal-Mart is trading at $50 a share, you earn $500 ($50 market price – $45 strike price). You must deduct from this profit, however, the initial cost of the option, which is nonrefundable.

If you purchased a put option and Wal-Mart shares declined a like amount, you would also profit. Put simply, when you buy an option, you are taking a point of view—higher or lower—within a give time frame, namely, the life of the option.

Option prices have two components: time value and intrinsic (sometimes called cash) value. Time value, as the name suggests, is that component of the price relating to how much time is left in the option prior to expiration. Hence, if this is January, an option with a July expiration is worth less than an option with identical terms scheduled to expire in September. This value, therefore, pertains to the amount of time left to expiration. A Wal-Mart July 45 call will always be lower in value than a Wal-Mart September 45 call. The cash component of the price applies to whether the options are said to be in the money. A 45 call is in the money by $1 if the stock is trading at $46 a share. The total value of the option will be comprised of both cash and time values. Hence, with 10 months to expiration, a July 45 call might be selling at $2 if the stock is at $46. That's $1 in cash value ($46 – $45 = $1) and $1 in time value.

There are many nuances to option pricing that a more complete discussion of this subject would cover. For instance, time value erodes at a much faster rate once expiration is about to occur. An option typically holds its time value and rapidly declines only as expiration becomes imminent. Consider an option that is said to be out of the money. With the market for the underlying Wal-Mart shares at, say, $43, the 45-strike calls have no cash value, only time value. The options will retain some value right up to the final day of trading in this instance. As a general rule, you want to buy options trading near the money—meaning 45-strike calls when the stock is at $44 or $43. When you buy options that are in the money, you are paying for value that already exists, thereby increasing your costs. With deeply out-of-the-money options—those with strike prices far from the market price—you are paying considerably less, but the opportunity for the option to ever prove profitable is far less. A stock that is trading at the strike price is said to be at the money.

GETTING STARTED IN OPTIONS TRADING

Options trading can be an extremely lucrative undertaking, but you must understand the risks involved. For most newcomers to the game, options might seem a dream come true. For a couple of thousand dollars, you can buy up options in Microsoft, Motorola, Disney, and even Google and profit in all the gains of the underlying stocks. And the potential profits can be dramatic. A few years ago, I was able to buy Disney call options for just $2 per option. Several months later, I sold the Disney calls for $10 each, a five-fold increase in my money! More often than not, however, the underlying shares don't move. This means the option buyer is looking at a loss of all the invested funds or at least a portion of those funds. You must always be cognizant of the risks involved when you buy options.

If option buying is risky, what about selling them? That's right, just like in the stock market, there is a seller for every buyer. Actually, one individual may sell thousands of options to many, many buyers. The one-to-one ratio is not important. What is important is that you recognize that someone is betting against you when you buy an option. The seller's job is to perform on the other end of the contract—namely, to provide you with stock at the strike price if you decide to exercise your option. As a practical matter, you will almost never actually exercise the option; nine times out of ten, you simply sell the option in the options market.

When you purchase a call, you purchase the right to buy the underlying stock at the strike price. The seller, therefore, must agree to provide you with that stock. You, the buyer, pay a premium to the seller for this privilege. The premium, therefore, is income to the seller of the option and a cost to the buyer. Regardless of what happens in the days subsequent to the sale of the option, the seller gets to keep the premium and therefore gets a fixed return for selling an option. When you first enter into this agreement to buy an option, the transaction is known as an opening transaction. When you decide to get out by selling the option, the transaction is known as a closing transaction. Once you have both bought and sold, the option ceases to exist. Likewise, from the seller's prospective, when he buys back his short position, his liability ceases to exist.

Now we have discussed how a buyer has a fixed cost and unlimited potential. What about the seller? The seller has the very opposite: a fixed and known income from selling the option and an unlimited liability since the underlying stock (in the case of a call option) can soar to infinity. Why, given these odds, sell options? Paradoxically enough, the seller often gets the better part of the deal. The seller has income whereas the buyer has an expense. The buyer, in order to profit, must see an appreciation in the price of the underlying security. If the stock doesn't move, the time value inevitably goes to zero. Most new option buyers expect the market to move. All too often, however, the stock languishes or goes in the other direction.

Finally, the seller must perform by posting good faith margin money with the broker on a day-to-day basis if the options sold prove profitable to the buyer. By seeing that the option is marked to the market daily, the trading exchanges ensure the integrity of all their contracts.

The one word that best applies to options is *versatile*. An unbelievable number of sophisticated strategies utilize options. You can use options to hedge your stock portfolio, for instance. If you own IBM shares and fear a downturn, you can buy IBM puts to protect yourself—and keep the stock to boot! You can spread options: buy one strike-price call and sell another strike-price call. These can be either bull or bear spreads and can be puts, calls, or both. You can spread options between expiration months, for example, buying July calls and selling September calls. You can do what are known as ratio writes, when you sell twice as many calls as you buy—or vice versa. All these strategies have their time and place. But the basic strategy is simply to buy calls when you think the market is about to rise and buy puts when you think lower prices are ahead.

There are options available today on a remarkable number of stocks and indexes, even commodities, precious metals, and petroleum futures. In the traditional stock options, you actually received the underlying stock. But if you prefer to trade a basket of stocks, you can buy options on the OEX S&P 100 traded at the Chicago Board Options Exchange and the popular S&P 500 index traded at the Chicago Mercantile Exchange. When you are dealing with stock indexes, there is no actual delivery of stock, only a cash payment at the end when the option actually becomes the cash index. These products were developed to help large institutional investors hedge their portfolios. Because of their enormous liquidity, they have gained a large following among small individual investors.

Looked at from its most basic strategy, call buying is the primary focus of most small investors. People don't like to bet that stocks are going down. For one, a stock can only fall to zero; for another, the potential of capturing a bonanza is far greater when you purchase calls. The cost of buying a call option is relatively small. The problem is, of course, that you must be correct not only about the direction the market or stock will take but also about its timing. While call buying can be very profitable, it can be frustrating in the sense that you can be correct on the stock but wrong on the timing. I can remember not so many years ago aggressively buying 10-strike calls on Motorola (MOT). The stock was struggling and couldn't stage the rally. Today, Motorola is trading above 20. But this is little consolation; the call options have long since expired, worthless. In looking back at this fiasco, I would have profited handsomely if I'd simply purchased the stock.

As you can see, there are clearly trade-offs when you decide to utilize options instead of stocks, or vice versa. There are pros and cons to each. But it probably won't hurt if you undertake a small option-buying program just to get your feet wet. There is nothing more likely to get your interest than having some money at risk. So consider buying several options to see how this strategy appeals to you. You don't have to commit a lot of money. With many good options trading below $5, your out-of-pocket expenses will be minimal.

HOW TO USE OPTION VOLUME TO PINPOINT MOVES

Option volume can sometimes be a very useful tool to spot stock moves. A significant increase in the option volume often signals an impending move higher or lower in the underlying security. This is because options offer enhanced leverage to the investor, who, anticipating an impending move, can use the options market to capitalize on the situation. Fortunately, this boost in volume is clearly evident to those who know how to spot this development in investor sentiment. Ask yourself this: If you knew an important development in a given security was imminent, would you utilize stock or options to maximize your gains? While options certainly have some drawbacks—such as reduced liquidity—the answer would most certainly favor puts or calls. Why? Because the leverage is so much greater with options. If you had a sure thing, you would buy options on account of the increased leverage.

Accordingly, astute investors routinely monitor option volume to find opportunities. Option volume is one reliable indicator that a company is about to make a market-moving announcement. This announcement might take the form of a takeover bid, enhanced or decreased earnings, a merger, or a settlement of a major lawsuit—just about anything that can cause a stock to soar or plummet. The key to finding the signal is monitoring the difference between average options volume versus increased options volume. The best online source for this vital information is Zacks.com from

Zacks Investment Research. This firm tracks both put and call volume and pinpoints those stocks that have unusually high put and call volume. The general rules for finding good candidates are simple:

- Excessively high call volume suggests higher prices in the underlying stock.
- Excessively high put volume suggests lower prices in the underlying stock.

Moreover, you want to at least double the normal volume to find a good candidate.

Before you begin looking at high-volume option candidates, however, you must be aware that some stocks simply attract high-volume option activity. There are other things you must know as well to rule out some stocks. You typically want the high volume to be spread out among all the stock's options, not just a single put or call option. There might be excessive arbitrage going on with a specific stock, and you don't want this hedging activity to mislead you into buying or selling the wrong stock. If most of the activity occurred in one call series, chances are an institution executed a sale of calls against stock that they own. This might indeed account for the high call volume.

Also, monitor the expiration months in which the heightened activity occurs. As a rule, speculators want to trade near-term options because there is less time value to pay for. The exception to this rule occurs when the option has less than 10 days left prior to expiration. In this instance, the speculators don't want the short period of time before expiration to negatively affect their opportunities for profit. What if a takeover bid is delayed? There may not be time for the situation to properly develop.

What if both put and call volume are increasing? In this instance, you have to look at the stock price to determine if prices are headed higher or lower.

Tables 8.1 and 8.2 and Figures 8.1 and 8.2 show examples of both puts and calls that have recently experienced enhanced volume activity.

TABLE 8.1 Calls

Stock	Recent Call Volume	Average Call Volume	Ratio
Intel	84,856	41,078	2.1
Advanced Micro Devices	69,271	25,600	2.7
Oracle	24,252	10,653	2.3
Osi Pharmaceuticals	14,773	3,616	4.1
Ciena Corp.	9,066	899	10.1

TABLE 8.2 Puts

Stock	Recent Put Volume	Average Put Volume	Ratio
Starbucks	30,146	5,016	6
Abercrombie & Fitch	25,850	4,046	6.4
Bank of America	29,352	11,536	2.5
iShares Nasdaq Biotechnology	14,498	3,682	3.9

The daily ratio number reflects the recent volume activity in terms of the monthly average.

Even a cursory glance at the subsequent price movement of the underlying stocks whose option volume is listed here shows that those stocks with heightened call volume experienced rising prices and those with heightened put volume experienced lower prices. Clearly, tracking the volume activities of the put and call market can have a favorable impact on your portfolio results.

THE RULES

You will do best if you follow a few simple rules. First, do your homework on the stocks you want to buy options on, just as if you were purchasing

FIGURE 8.1 Surge in Call Volume Signals Higher Prices Ahead for Ciena Corp.

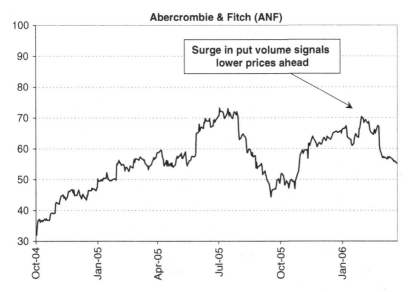

FIGURE 8.2 Surge in Put Volume Signals Lower Prices Ahead for Abercrombie & Fitch

the stock. Your financial commitment with options may not be great, but you want to have the odds favoring you. Remember, options are a wasting asset, so you need news, earnings, or some dramatic event to affect your option price. Second, limit your option activities to one type of strategy. By this, I mean choosing option buying as opposed to option selling, spreading, or any number of sophisticated strategies beyond the scope of this book. You want to be a specialist in the area you are trading. You might want, for instance, to concentrate on buying options in the technology sector, or medical stocks, or whatever. When you know a stock or sector well, you have a better feel for its rhythm and movement.

I mentioned this before, but you want to buy options that are trading at or near the money. If it is a $63 stock, you want to buy the 65-strike calls. If the option is a little out of the money, fine; deep out-of-the-money options, however, have a tough time becoming profitable. Remember that time is your enemy when you buy options; you need movement before the expiration of the option. Select options that have expiration dates three to six months in the future. When you buy near-term options, you must have lightning strike; when you buy long-term options, you are paying too much for time value. Three to six months seems about right. If this is April, look for July or September expirations. You can always roll into the December options several months down the road.

Take profits! A quick double in option value should have you taking profits. You'd be surprised how fast an option can soar in value when a stock runs. Take some profits, and let others ride.

Take losses! If you buy an option and it suddenly loses half its value, you have probably made a mistake. Take the loss and move on.

Stay with the liquid options. You want the options you trade to have many buyers and sellers. When you lack liquidity, you'll have trouble finding a willing buyer or seller to take the other side of your trade.

I remember several months back looking at Apple Computer. The stock had traded up from $45 to $60 a share, a nice $15 profit in just three months. At the time, a $6,000 investment in Apple would have bought you 100 shares. But at the same time, an out-of-the-money 65-strike Apple call could have been had for less than a buck. Trending higher, the $6,000 stock investment would have been worth approximately $8,500 three months later. But the same investment in 65-strike calls would have been worth approximately $150,000 during the same time period! When option players claim to get more bang for the buck, they aren't kidding. Options can give you the edge to make serious money.

There are many other examples of options that posted spectacular returns to their buyers. In the Apple example, you have to ask yourself if you are willing to risk losing your entire investment, however. Had Apple share prices topped out at $60 and not risen to $86, the entire option investment might have been lost. Nevertheless, an option-buying program might be worth trying with at least a portion of your investment funds. The general rule is that most options expire worthless. That means the sellers, or writers, of the options get to keep the premiums as profits and the buyers lose. For this very reason, you must be careful when you purchase puts or calls. But the occasional bonanzas to be made in option trading make them an attractive speculative vehicle. This is especially true when you consider that option buying enables you to participate in the potential gains of higher-priced stocks that would be out of reach to the average small investor.

CHAPTER 9

Your Roadmap for Success Tomorrow

N ot long ago, on a visit to my Canadian summer home, I opened the morning newspaper to be greeted by a huge headline: "The $444-million Boulder." Labeled "the gold strike of the decade," the article, which immediately caught my attention, went on:

*Andre Gaumond, who this week agreed to sell his junior exploration company to **Goldcorp Inc.** for $443.8 million, can trace his good fortune back to a quirky, two-tonne boulder that seemed out of place in Quebec's James Bay lowlands.*

The article went on to describe how CEO Gaumond and a team of geologists had stumbled upon "one of the most significant gold discoveries in recent memory." My jaw dropped when I read the name of Gaumond's company: **Virginia Gold Mines, Inc.** This was the very same company whose shares I had purchased for $1 Canadian (about 76 cents U.S. at the time) just a few short years ago. The current price: $15.28! See Figure 9.1.

Exploration drilling had started in September 2004, and now, just over a year later, the company was being bought out at a huge premium. Being modest, the CEO pointed out that luck in discovering gold was part of the game. The background on the company's efforts, however, revealed a total of $40 million in underwriting efforts and four previous mines that didn't yield a profit. The fifth mine was the bonanza. To illustrate how potentially lucrative this find was, the most recent discovery revealed gold grades of 10 grams per ton. By comparison, the most significant discovery in the previous 25 years was only 4 grams per ton. The fact that gold recently traded

167

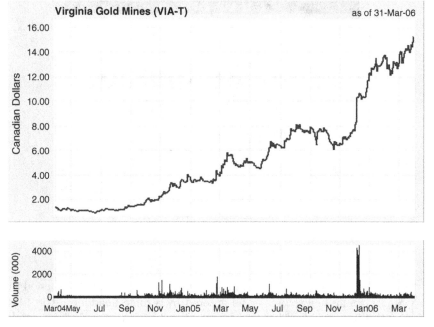

FIGURE 9.1   Virginia Gold Mines, Inc., Jumps
Source: Courtesy of the Toronto Stock Exchange.

over $1,000 an ounce, the highest price in recent memory, made the find that much more attractive.

I know what you are thinking. How do you find companies like this one? Well, if the CEO thinks that luck played a significant factor, chances are it did. But there's a checklist of possibilities that might provide a glimpse of similar candidates when you are out prospecting for hot stocks.

BUY WHEN STOCKS ARE LOW-PRICED AND DEPRESSED

Stocks that eventually become big winners often start out low-priced and out of favor. The problem, however, rests with the meaning of low-priced, depressed, and so on. A company selling for a dollar may be way over-priced, and a $30 stock might be undervalued.

As a rule, you want to buy when there is the proverbial blood in the streets. Investor psychology tends to militate against this strategy. The average investor or Wall Street pundit wants to buy a story stock, not some dog that hasn't seen its day.

When looking for some guidelines in selecting a winning candidate, you must consider the importance of contrary opinion theory: In a nutshell, most people will be wrong. If you select popular stocks, therefore, you are likely to be late to the game, and the chances favoring price appreciation are slim. Given time, the out-of-favor stocks will typically earn their popularity, but by that juncture, you want to be selling, not buying.

Specifically, avoid stocks that have already run. In such situations, the stock's story is already known. Rather, be a contrarian, and look for a stock that has already come down 45 to 65 percent off its prior highs. This shows that profit-taking has already beaten the stock lower and that, perhaps, investors are experiencing second thoughts about the company's prospects. Ideally, you will have a turnaround situation or a company whose prospects are tied to resources in the ground or a new technology that can propel the stock's price higher once it becomes known. If one of these scenarios pans out, you will have a winner.

The easiest way to spot a good opportunity is to continually study price charts, lots of them. With only a cursory glance, you will be able to tell whether a stock is soaring higher (too late to buy) or dormant and perhaps ready to soar. Look for increasing volume; a stock on the most active list may be getting ready to run. But you want to get aboard before the stock runs, not after.

If you can identify a turnaround situation, you must be patient. A turnaround can take a year and a half to two and a half years. But if you select the right stock, the wait will be worth it.

If you want a ready illustration, look at a price chart of Covad Communications (DVW) in Figure 9.2. Here's a stock that simply tumbled for months on end. Then it recently gained 41 percent in value on merger news in one day!

Look at Northern Orion (NTO) in Figure 9.3, which was formerly limited to trading on the Toronto Exchange and now trades at the Amex. The stock lost more than a third of its value earlier in the year and then gained it all back.

In Flextronics (FLEX) in Figure 9.4, the stock lost 25 percent of its value before recovering the entire move. It then lost an even greater percentage of its worth (about 40 percent), but it is once again poised to move higher.

RF Micro Devices (RFMD) lost two-thirds of its value in the past two years, falling to $4 from a high of $12. But in recent months, the stock is on the mend. See Figure 9.5.

A stock can be like a mile-long freight train. It takes time to slow its trajectory and move in the opposite direction. We are looking for at least

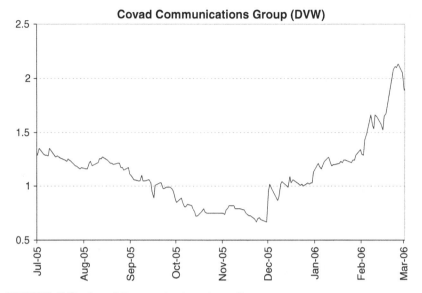

FIGURE 9.2   Covad Communications Price Chart

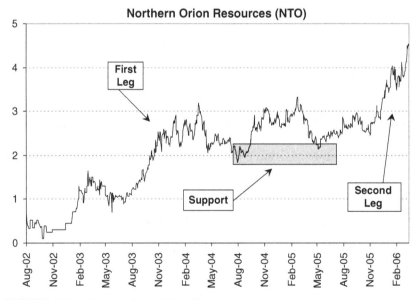

FIGURE 9.3   Northern Orion Price Chart

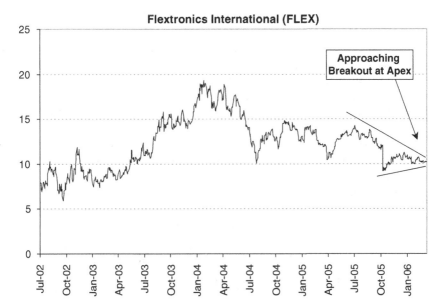

FIGURE 9.4 Flextronics Price Chart

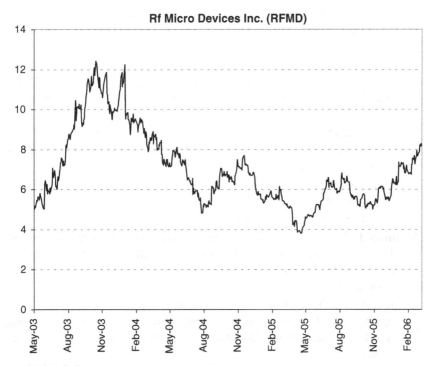

FIGURE 9.5 RF Micro Devices Price Chart

18 months before the results of a legitimate turnaround are reflected in a stock's price. The silver lining in this often painful process is that the subsequent rally is often commensurate with its decline.

There is a classic story about the investment legend John Templeton, who, back in 1939, instructed his broker to buy 100 shares of every listed stock selling below a dollar. His buying spree yielded shares in approximately 104 companies, resulting in a $10,000 investment. There were a fair number of dogs among the companies he purchased, including 34 companies that were in bankruptcy. Yet four years later, he was able to sell his entire stake for approximately $40,000—four times the cost of his investment.

Note that he held the shares for four years. Yet the story illustrates the importance of buying low-priced bargains and giving them time to grow. In keeping with this philosophy, let's define our rules as follows:

1. Buy only low-priced stocks that have been beaten down.
2. Be prepared to hold the stock at least 18 months.

Here are several candidates that fit our criteria:

Sirius Satellite Radio (SIRI): A booming company with enormous potential, Sirius enjoys tremendous activity and has taken every selloff in stride.

Capstone Turbine (CPST): This stock has already demonstrated its ability to trade higher, as evidenced from its rise from $1 to $5.50 a share. Beaten down to $1.50 a share, a move back to its old highs would bring at least $2 of profit.

Sonus Networks (SONS): This stock has lost almost half its value twice in the past two years. It is now poised for another run to the top of its range, and perhaps beyond.

ATS Medical (ATSI): This stock has been steadily losing value for two years now. With half its value gone and the stock trading near 52-week lows, the company is ripe for a turnaround.

Attunity Ltd. (ATTU): Out of favor and trading well down from its highs, this stock is another issue thrown on the junk pile. Should you buy what is being thrown away? Give it six months, and you will know the answer.

Broadvision (BVSN): Down to just 50 cents from almost $3 a share a year ago, this stock has lost over 70 percent of its value in the past six months. Hidden within this almost hopeless situation is the potential for gain.

Coeur d'Alene Mines (CDE): This company, which is benefiting from the rise in the price of precious metals, is clearly on the rise after being driven down by profit-taking earlier last year. Less than 70 cents below its 52-week high, the stock is poised to trade above $5 in the next six months.

IDENTIFY FIRST LEG AND COUNTERMOVE

The surest sign that a market wants to move is a strong first leg, followed by a countermove. What do I mean by first leg? Look for a rally from an identifiable low to an identifiable high. This pattern inevitably comes after a breakout. Stocks typically rise in a symmetrical fashion. The first leg is a sign that the stock wants to rise; the countermove signals profit-taking. The second leg tends to parallel the first leg in both time and price. For example, XYZ stock suddenly rises from, say, $4 to $7, or 3 points. At $7, the stock encounters profit-taking, knocking the price down to $5.25, where prices stabilize. You then have a so-called consolidation period or sideways action. On the next rally, the stock should reach $8.25. Why $8.25? Because $8.25 is exactly 3 points above the equilibrium point of $5.25. And since the first leg had a magnitude of 3 points, the likelihood is that the second leg will parallel this move.

What's amazing about this time and price philosophy is that markets often rise in a symmetrical fashion not only related to price but also to time. So if the breakout phase resulted in a six-day rally, chances are the second run to the top (after the consolidation phase) will also be six days in duration.

I've written extensively on this subject in my book *Sniper Trading* (John Wiley & Sons, 2002). But here I've presented the time and price philosophy in a nutshell.

Now, for the nuts and bolts. In prospecting for winning candidates, you must let the stock tell you it wants to run. How do you identify the right stock? You monitor a list of stocks and look for one that has recently made a substantial gain. Once you identify the stock, you do *not* buy the stock. Rather, you wait for the inevitable pullback to occur. In the meantime, you measure the time and price of the stock, the basic dimensions of the first leg. Specifically, what was the magnitude of the move, and what was the duration of the move? Once the stock retreats in price, you look for signs of support. You then purchase the stock at the support.

When the inevitable second rally (or leg) occurs, you then sell out the position at the anticipated sell target, information you will know by measuring the first leg.

The best way to visualize this pattern is looking at an example. Using round numbers, look at a two-year chart of Sirius Satellite Radio (SIRI). Between September 2004 and January 2005, the satellite radio stock made a sharp rally from approximately $2 to $8, a 6-point gain. During the balance of 2005, the stock consolidated in the $6 to $7 area, forming a strong support. When the inevitable breakout to the upside occurs on the next leg, the stock should reach $14 to $15, based on the time and price numbers. Moreover, the rally should take approximately four months to be completed.

Now this is a long-term view of the stock. And the breakout to new high ground may not occur until three to six months in the future—or even a year from now. But the probabilities favor the move and the target sell price.

Looking at a shorter-term chart of the same stock, you should be able to identify many more short-term rallies and counterrallies. For example, during the fall of 2005, Sirius rose off its October lows (a great month to buy stock) from approximately $5.80 to the 52-week high of $7.98 in December. This rally of 2.18 points was followed by the inevitable profit-taking, which pushed the stock down below $7. It stabilized between $7 and $6.50. From a short-term perspective, the stock should rally another $2.18. The sell target—depending on what number you want to use as the support—is approximately $8.98 to $9.15. Again, this is a short-term sell target (based on short-term data), as opposed to the more generous outlook suggested by the longer-term data.

To start performing your own analysis tomorrow, follow these seven simple rules:

1. Identify a low-priced stock that has recently rallied.
2. Measure the move from low to high.
3. Measure the move in terms of duration: 28 days, 5 weeks, 9 months, or whatever.
4. Look for a pullback to the support level.
5. Add the length of the first leg to the support level to pinpoint selling target price.
6. Add the number of days, weeks, or months of the first leg to the low of the support level date to identify potential top day.
7. Buy stock.

If this sounds like a lot of work, it isn't. These calculations become routine once you do them on a regular basis. For example:

RF Micro Devices (RFMD): This stock rallied from approximately $4 to $6.50 before pulling back to $5.00. The target, based on the first leg, is $7.50. See Figure 9.6.

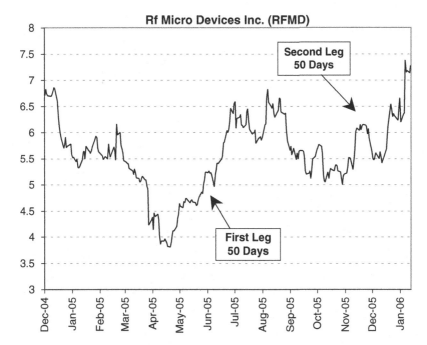

FIGURE 9.6 RF Micro Devices Rallies

Desert Sun Mining (DEZ): This stock has made a sustained, 10-month rally during 2005 from approximately $1 to $6.50. Since the first leg is not yet complete, it is too early to buy. But once profit-taking occurs, this should take off. See Figure 9.7.

DRDGold (DROOY): From April to December 2005, this stock created a first leg from 70 cents to $1.90. It later pulled back to $1.25. Currently trading near $1.40, the second leg should carry at least to $2.60. See Figure 9.8.

Lucent Technology (LU): Lucent established a $1 leg between $2.35 and $3.35 last year. Having pulled back to $2.50, the second leg should take the stock to $3.50 within the next few months. See Figure 9.9.

Northgate Minerals (NXG): Having made a sustained rally from $1.30 to $2.50 since November 2005, this stock has yet to experience profit-taking, so it is too early to buy. But the first pullback should be a buying opportunity. See Figure 9.10.

Bema Gold (BGO): This was a true penny stock that entered the big leagues. The stock rose from $1 to $4 in 2003 and has since been consolidating. Trading near $3 a share, the top should be at $6. See Figure 9.11.

FIGURE 9.7 Desert Sun Mining Rallies

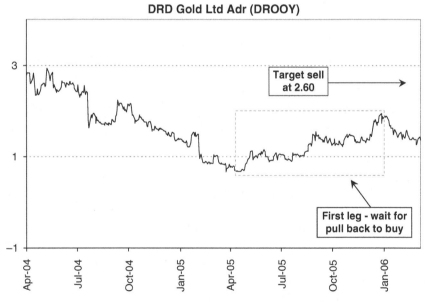

FIGURE 9.8 DRDGold Rallies

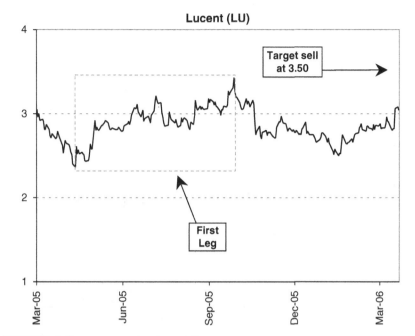

FIGURE 9.9 Lucent Technology Rallies

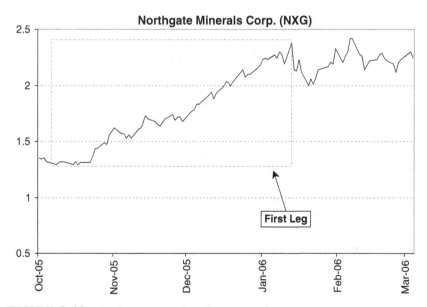

FIGURE 9.10 Northgate Minerals Rallies

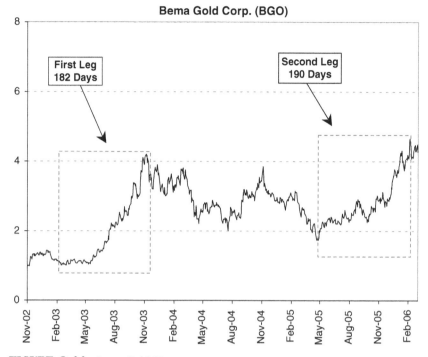

FIGURE 9.11 Bema Gold Rises

THE WORST-PERFORMING ISSUES

The best future returns are often found among the worst-performing issues. Accordingly, put these poor performers on your watch list. Just remember that it may take some time for the turnaround situation to manifest itself in solid stock gains. In a recent issue of *Investor's Business Daily*, the following stocks were cited as performing poorly:

- Pier 1 (PIR)
- Arrhythmia Research Technology (HRT)
- Nucryst Pharmaceuticals (NCST)
- Tofutti Brands (TOF)
- TRX, Inc. (TRXI)
- Navious Maritime (NM)
- Velocity Express (VEXPS)
- Engex (EGX)

All these companies are at or near their 52-week lows, and their respective prospects seem grim. Ironically, this is precisely where you are likely to find an enormous percent gainer in the months ahead. The best future returns tend to rise from among the worst of the past returns. Out-of-favor issues such as these often register gains that are nothing short of sensational. Stocks that you cannot give away are often extremely desirable as they approach new highs months later. Moreover, don't be surprised if one of these stocks spends considerable time at its lows. This is classic base building, a necessary phenomenon that must occur prior to a surge in prices. Admittedly, not every stock will rise like the phoenix out of the ashes. But those that do will clearly outpace the Microsofts and other blue chips once they gain their strength and begin to rally.

ALWAYS BUY AT SUPPORT

Support, which is defined as an area where buyers step in and prevent a stock from falling below a certain level, is always a good place to buy a stock. A support level may exist from several weeks ago or even several months or years ago. The point is that stocks return to support levels more often than most investors would think.

To get started on finding a good investment candidate tomorrow, simply look back at a company's price action. Where was the previous support? Is the stock price approaching that price right now? If not, does it show any likelihood of reaching prior support? These are all questions that can help you make an intelligent decision concerning support.

Remember the classic rules concerning support. Prior resistance *becomes* support once it is penetrated. That means the new support (where you will buy) is at the point where you would have previously sold. Confused? Don't be. This is a simple concept. Let's look at a few examples that will make the selection process easier for you.

Liveperson Inc. (LPSN): Trading near $5.50, this stock has strong support above $5. See Figure 9.12.

Novavax Inc. (NVAX): Novavax based with strong support at $3, which is the logical buying target. It is unlikely to trade down to that level, however. See Figure 9.13.

Sun Microsystems, Inc. (SUNW): Tightly wound, Sun has formed a strong base first at $3.50 and now $4.00 (the prior resistance). With the stock trading at $5.00, the $4 area would be the logical place to buy the stock *if* it trades that low before taking off to the upside. See Figure 9.14.

Golden Star Resources (GSS): With mines in Ghana and a successful recent influx of cash from an equity offering, Golden Star is poised to move higher. The stock has support just above $3. See Figure 9.15.

FIGURE 9.12   Liveperson Inc.

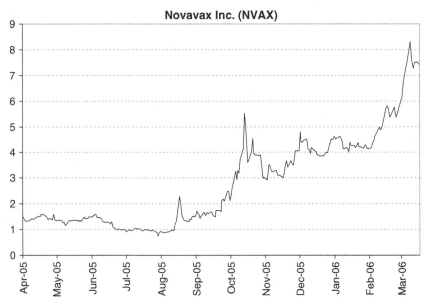

FIGURE 9.13   Novavax Inc.

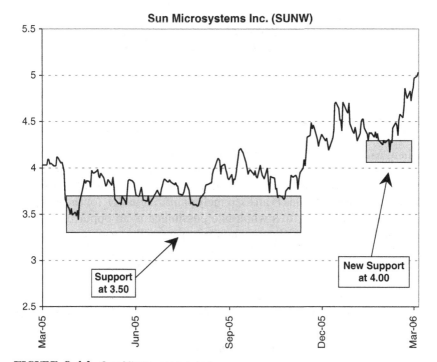

FIGURE 9.14 Sun Microsystems, Inc.

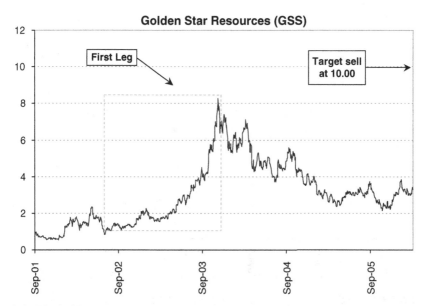

FIGURE 9.15 Golden Star Resources

In these examples, we are not trying to buy stocks at their lows—only identify where support might exist. The idea is to buy into a rising trend but at a point where the risk is low. The support is the area where you will have a low-risk buying opportunity.

PRICE CAPITULATION

When, as occasionally happens, support fails, you have what is known in technical analysts' circles as price capitulation. This occurs when all hope is lost and conventional wisdom dictates that shareholders abandon their positions. Obviously, this is an extremely painful situation for the investors. But to the contrarian, this wholesale pessimism is an opportunity. Price capitulation is an easy phenomenon to observe. Prices plummet on high volume. The contrarian uses this as an opportunity to purchase shares at bargain-basement prices. Consider the following recent examples:

Bema Gold (BGO): As shown in Figure 9.16, this is the classic example of a stock that experienced price capitulation, only to soar immediately

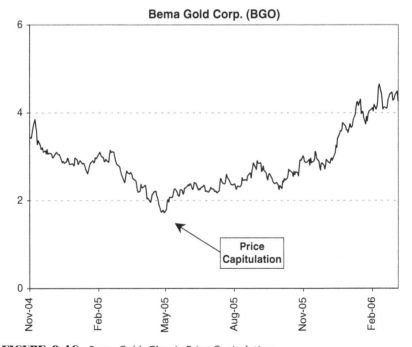

FIGURE 9.16 Bema Gold: Classic Price Capitulation

afterward. On May 23, 2005, Bema fell to $1.70 a share on high volume. A month later, the stock had gained 37 percent in value, soaring to $2.33 a share on June 23, 2005. By the following January, the stock traded at a new 52-week high of $3.85 a share.

ON2 Technologies (ONT): This stock exhibited strong support at 60 cents, but on August 15, 2005, ON2 fell to 52 cents, breaking the support. Less than five months later, the stock had gained a whopping 183 percent in value, jumping to new highs at $1.48 a share. For bottom-fishers playing the price capitulation game, this was an impressive payoff. See Figure 9.17.

Sun Microsystems (SUNW): This price reversal was an easy one to spot because the stock traded a whopping 153.5 million shares on the day following the low of the year. See Figure 9.18. Normal volume in Sun is just 48.5 million shares, so the tripling of the volume was the clue that the downside move was over. Since the April 28, 2005, low was made at $3.42, the stock gained over a dollar in value by year's end.

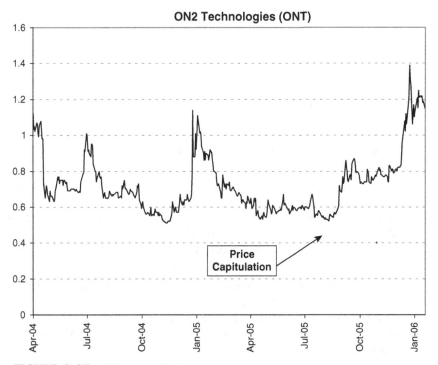

FIGURE 9.17 ON2 Technologies

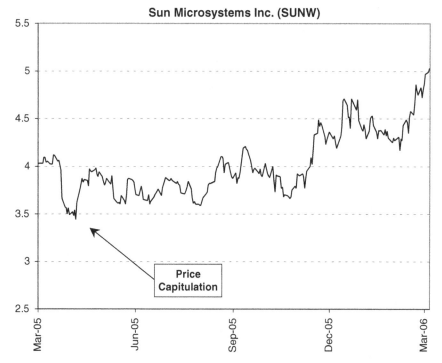

FIGURE 9.18   Sun Microsystems

Sirius Satellite Radio (SIRI): More than five times the average volume of
16.4 million shares traded in Sirius on April 27, 2005, the day it registered its yearly low at $4.42 a share. The price capitulation suggested
the downward move was over. It has since powered its way back up to
the $6.50 a share area. See Figure 9.19.

Pelangio Mines (PLG.TO): This Toronto Exchange–traded mining company registered more than four times the average normal volume on
June 8, 2005, when it registered its 52-week lows at just 30 cents a
share. Within six months, the shares doubled in value and then hit new
highs in early January 2006. When the crowd sells, buy! Pelangio recently made new highs close to $3 a share. See Figure 9.20.

Conexant Systems (CNXT): When Conexant shares fell under a dollar in
early May 2005, investors gave up. The volume on May 4, 2005, was
24.7 million, more than double the average 10.4 million shares that the
stock normally trades. The low made on that day was 95 cents. See
Figure 9.21.

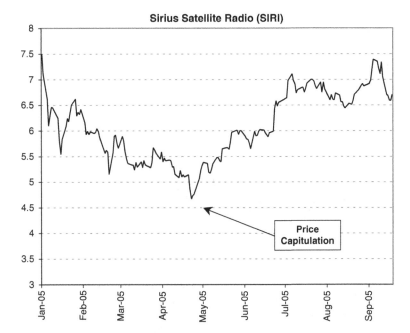

FIGURE 9.19 Sirius Satellite Radio

FIGURE 9.20 Pelangio Mines
Source: Courtesy of the Toronto Stock Exchange.

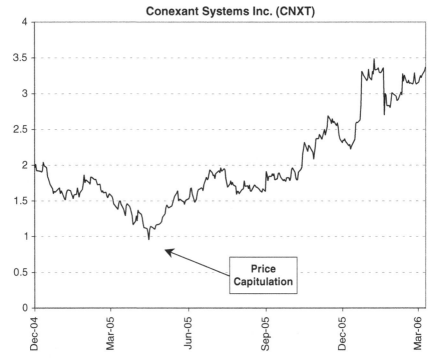

FIGURE 9.21 Conexant Systems

As these examples illustrate, the mob psychology is to give up at the bottom. Learn to see price capitulation for what it is—an opportunity—and you won't be left without shares in a rising market.

If you are going to be successful in finding profitable opportunities, you must be willing to look for the market panics that frequently occur when a stock becomes too oversold. These panics are driven by emotion, pure and simple. Whatever the underlying fundamentals of the company, the selloffs at the bottom, and corresponding blow-offs at the top, are never entirely warranted. For the investor looking for a good opportunity, panics can be a valuable clue as to when to purchase a stock. Remember the tenets of contrary opinion: The mob is always wrong at the major turns. This is never truer than when the bottom falls out of a market.

Take the case of Nxstage Medical (NXTM), a Massachusetts-based medical device–making company with no history of earning profits. As shown in Figure 9.22, the stock slid steadily from $14.80 a share to $9 a share over several months. On news that a Merrill Lynch analyst was raising the rating on the stock, Nxstage surged 14 percent in value in a single

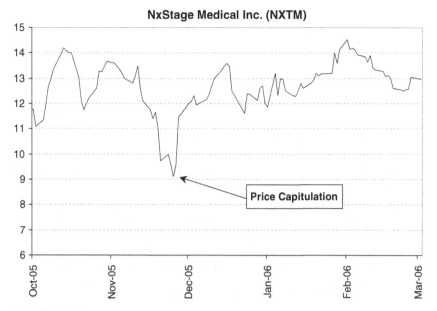

Nxstage Medical Inc. (NXTM)

Price Capitulation

FIGURE 9.22 When the Bottom Falls Out: NxStage Medical

day on above-average volume. The analyst noted that the company, which he expects to be profitable in 2008, was trading at a "significant discount" at $9. His target: $16 a share. (The high actually proved to be $15.61 a share.) Sometimes that is all it takes to create a turnaround in a stock's price. The stock surged despite the anticipation of continued losses over the next two years. The point: The losses will be diminishing and the company, in time, will be profitable. In a two-week period recently, the stock gained over 44 percent in value.

When a stock is ready to run, it is amazing how quickly the fundamentals can change. I own a stock that recently gained 20 percent in value in a single day on a strong press release pointing to future profits. Prior to the PR, the company couldn't do anything right, according to investor sentiment. The shares were sent to new 52-week lows. This precise scenario was being played out.

The hallmark of a truly hopeless stock that is about to surge higher is total gloom on the fundamental front. Look for continued red ink on the bottom line and a management that has lost all credibility with the investing public and the analytical community. Such widespread pessimism will almost certainly drive the stock price lower. As a rule, this negativism becomes a self-fulfilling event as stop-loss orders are hit and the public gives up. At this point, professional traders, who have probably been monitoring the situation right along, rush in with buy orders—and you are off to the races. The stock may break higher on a gap. At this stage, the trajectory is clearly higher.

DEVELOPING A WINNING MIND-SET

Believe it or not, developing a way to find winning stocks is not enough. You have to know how to handle winners. I've been giving my friends winning stock tips for years, but precious few of them have ever made any money. The reason: My unsolicited advice has frequently fallen on deaf ears. For whatever reason, even a written selection of winning stocks is insufficient for many people to make money. You know the reasons: I don't have any money to invest right now. It looks too high (low) to me. I think I will watch the market for a while (and then the stock soars out of sight). I want to be cautious, so I will only purchase 500 shares. There are a million excuses why genuine opportunities are missed in the market.

Investing can be a painful experience. You can lose money. And nothing is more demoralizing than losing money in the market. At least when you go to Las Vegas and lose money, you can always say you had a good time. To develop the correct attitude toward the market, you must develop winning habits. The most important—not to say profitable—habit is to become a consistent winner. How do you do this? Not by winning on every trade. The probability of never selecting a losing stock is extremely low. I've already told you that I've had more than my share of stocks that managed to go to zero. Ironically, some of the bankruptcy stories result in companies that emerge from the ashes in reorganization and go on to make money, but not before the shareholders' equity has been wiped out. The opportunity for disaster is always present when you invest money in the stock market.

For winning traders who embrace the risk, however, the gains and losses are just part of the game. They know they are operating in a risky environment, but they also know that, over time, they are playing a winning game—one they can capitalize on by utilizing sound strategies.

For example, winning traders want to take profits when they become available. This is in opposition to the theory that you overstay a market and watch your investment go sour. Indeed, some of my best profits came from stocks that later went to zero—long after I'd taken profits. You can learn to do this by taking at least some profits when they become available. Let's say you buy a stock at $1 and it goes to $2. At $2, you have doubled your money. By taking off half of your position, you have a risk-free trade. If prices subsequently go lower, you have broken even. If prices continue higher, you make the difference at no risk.

You want to get yourself in a state of mind that will reward you again and again. The best way to do this is to make money over and over again. By doing this, you won't be prone to make mistakes resulting from your fear of losing. The psychological aspects of investing are among the more important, but least talked about, features of investing. When you see an opportunity (such as a stock making new lows), do you freeze and decide to watch the market for a while? Or do you follow your instincts by taking on the risks that others are fleeing? Remember, most investors (especially at the major turns) are wrong.

Can you accept the risks of investing? Or does the fear of losing money make you insist on a sure thing?

A lot of people define their investment strategy as a battle. It is a battle, but not between you and the market. It is a battle between your emotions of negative expectation and your willingness to accept a world of abundance. When you expect good things, they often happen.

I don't know if you have ever experienced this phenomenon, but have you ever noticed that when you really, really need money, you can never make any? When you are carefree and not much worrying about making money, on the other hand, it often falls into your lap unannounced. I have witnessed this many times over the years, and I suspect it is a universal rule. When you stop worrying about money, you can start making real money. Over the years, I've witnessed just about every mistake a person can make in the market. Indeed, I've made most of them myself. But the people who manage to survive always have a way of putting their fears aside and moving toward their investment goals without really thinking about the money.

The market is totally indifferent to your particular stake in a given stock at any one time. The market is going to do what it is going to do regardless of its impact on you. It is not out to get you; on the contrary, it could care less. So who is the culprit when you lose money? Most likely, it is your own psychological shortcomings. Most of these have to do with simple human nature. No one enjoys losing money. So in the market, when you have a golden opportunity to purchase a stock, what do you do? You often watch the stock until it soars out of sight, and then you decide to buy at the top. Or like the countless millions who lost money in the last bubble, you tried to get in on the bandwagon at the very top! After all, at that point everyone knew the market was heading higher. Remember, the market is always the most bullish at the top and always the most bearish at the bottom. To make money, however, you must do the very opposite of what your emotions are telling you to do. You must sell tops and buy bottoms.

Although this point may be obvious, you'd be surprised how very difficult it is to do the right thing in the market. Of course, you want to buy low and sell high. Everyone else wants to do that as well. But can you accomplish that elusive goal?

One sure-fire way to cut down on the anxiety of worrying about which stock to buy and which way the market is headed is, ironically, to simply stop trying to predict the future. The fact is that you don't know what will happen to a particular company tomorrow, nor do you know how the news will affect a stock you own. The best way to capitalize on this lack of knowledge is to simply allow events to play out. You do this by buying stocks over and over again that offer good potential reward for the risks that you are willing to incur. For example, when you strive to be safe by purchasing a sure-thing winner such as a Microsoft or a General Motors, you are betting on continued success. But as we've seen in the automotive business in recent years, investing in an American automotive manufacturer is not exactly a safe investment. By taking a chance on innovative entrepreneurship, a new technology that promises to change the lives of millions, or even a given resource in the ground, you take a leap into the unknown where the rewards are uncertain but could be substantial. Ironically, the best investment is often the most uncertain. Betting on a sure thing, on the other hand, is comparable to knowing the winning numbers of the lottery—after the drawing has been held. The word is out. But it is too late.

The psychological pitfalls of investing are beyond the scope of this book, but you would do well to monitor your investing activities and then go back and analyze where you went wrong. Most investors, frankly, don't want to do this. They don't want to accept responsibility for their own mistakes. If you've ever looked at some of the bulletin boards for stocks, you'll see that most investors want someone to blame when their investments go awry. They want to blame management, or they want to blame those who post negative information or the people who pump up a stock by overstating the facts. The one thing they don't want to do is accept responsibility.

When you are thinking about purchasing or selling a stock, you must be aware that there are only three groups of people you must be concerned about: one, you have those who believe that prices are too low and the stock represents a relative bargain; two, you have those who think the stock is overvalued and due for a fall; three, you have those people who are waiting to make up their minds. This last group can tip the scales in your favor or against you. The problem is that it is difficult and not very productive to try to analyze the thoughts of those many undecided individuals. A stock price, therefore, can be in balance between buyers and sellers one day, only to soar or tank the next. It is as if hundreds of people were gathered on the deck of a ship and suddenly, everyone rushed to one side. Depending on the size of the vessel, the ship might capsize. Markets are like that. Things can change in a hurry. Your task is to be cognizant of these potential imbalances and attempt to capitalize on them when you can.

I've spent a lot of time focusing on low-priced and often out-of-favor stocks, some of these breaking to new low ground. That's because I firmly believe that the best opportunities are often found among the dispossessed stocks. Arguably, there are opportunities everywhere in the investment world. Low-priced stocks represent just one niche.

AN INVESTOR'S CHECKLIST

There are no correct answers to the 14 questions that follow. They are meant solely to alert you to the considerations every investor must make in selecting, placing, and exiting a winning position. As you go through the list, try to define your goals and concerns. I hope these questions will prompt you to fine-tune your investment style and pinpoint those areas where you need work.

1. *Is your potential stock trading near its 52-week lows—or is it soaring on investor enthusiasm?* This year's favorite stocks tend to underperform in the future. You are more likely to find a winner among those

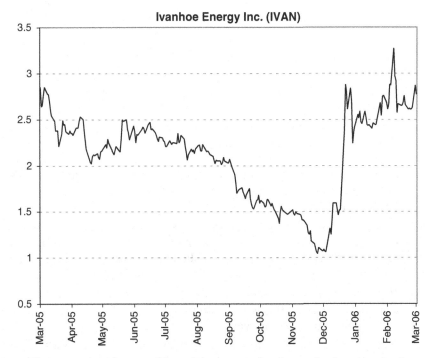

When a stock makes new 52-week lows, you often have a buying opportunity.

stocks making new lows. Look at the shares of Ivanhoe Energy (IVAN). Over a period of months, the stock slid from about $2.40 a share to a dollar. Then, virtually overnight, the stock went to $2.80 a share.

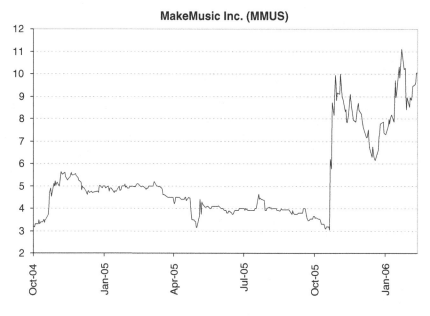

MakeMusic Inc. (MMUS)

2. *Are you buying during October, traditionally a low point during the year?* The odds favor a stock purchase made during October because the seasonal lows tend to be registered in the stock market in this month.

3. *Has your stock recently experienced capitulation?* This is an easy question to answer because many stocks will not rise until they have first killed every last believer in higher prices. Look for a gap down on enormous volume. When the stock makes new 52-week lows on this technical pattern, the down move is finally over. Look to buy on the first opportunity.

4. *Has your potential stock recently gapped higher?* You have no time to waste. You must buy the stock immediately. When a stock gaps up out of a consolidation, it is often a so-called breakaway gap, meaning the stock is ready to run.

5. *Has your stock recently created a first leg—and has it retraced a portion of its move?* If this is the pattern you are looking at, you have a golden opportunity before you.

6. *Can you identify the support price?* If so, what is the support? What is the current price? What is the risk?

7. *What is your company's financial position?* Is the company making money? Or at the very least, are the losses decreasing, suggesting profitability is on the horizon? You have to be a bit of a financial sleuth to analyze a company's financial statement. But you want to see a healthy cash flow down the road, lest the company's fortunes—and inevitably the stock price—head south.

   Is your company in a turnaround situation? If so, what makes you think so? New management? New products? An emerging technology? Are you prepared to hold the stock for the two or two-and-a-half years that a turnaround usually requires? These can be some of the most profitable situations, but they require patience.

8. *Has your stock been discovered by the press?* If so, chances are you have already missed the move. Widely publicized stocks rarely make the moves experienced by unknown stocks. This is not to say you don't want your stock to someday become a highly publicized stock, but by that time, you want to think about selling the stock and taking the profit you have already earned by buying early. Here's a stock I bet you have never heard of, at least not until lately: MakeMusic (MMUS). Six months ago, you could have bought all you wanted at $6 share. Today's price is just under $10.

9. *Can you identify bottoming patterns on the charts?* Stocks that are about to move higher often form bottoming patterns on the charts.

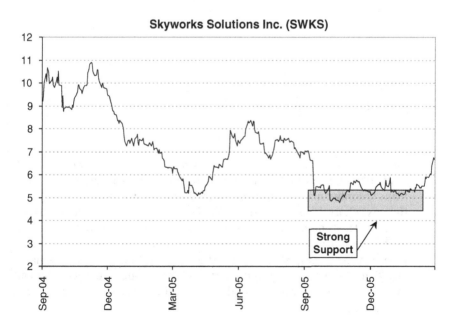

Skyworks Solutions Inc. (SWKS)

There are saucer bottoms and consolidation zones with clear-cut support and resistance. If a stock has spent six to nine months going sideways, it has probably formed a powerful bottoming action. Look at the double bottom formed on the chart for Skyworks Solutions (SWKS). This is a stock that now wants to move higher.

10. *Is your stock a potential asset play?* If so, what is the asset? Do you have reason to believe the demand for that asset will rise? Take a look at Tanzanian Royalty Exploration (TRE). This Vancouver-based gold-mining company, with properties in Africa, has a three-year range of 72 cents to over $7. Clearly, the recent boom in gold prices, the company's chief product, has resulted in higher share prices.

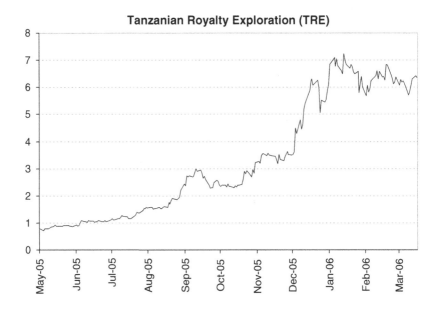

11. *Can you point to several indicators all suggesting higher prices?* Typically, one chart pattern is not sufficient to constitute a signal. You want a confluence of indicators all pointing in the same direction. In the next chart, Ivanhoe Energy (IVAN) has seen its stock almost triple in price. The fundamental news that propelled the stock was all bullish, as it sealed promising natural gas deals in both California and the Far East. On the technical side, both the slow- and fast-stochastics have significant crossovers on the chart, and a number of other technical indicators were deeply oversold. The inevitable bounce occurred and the stock soared.

12. *Have you performed the analysis of the stock's strength by calculating the five-day oscillator numbers?* This simple calculation is based on recent range numbers. It can pinpoint buying strength before the stock starts to move higher.

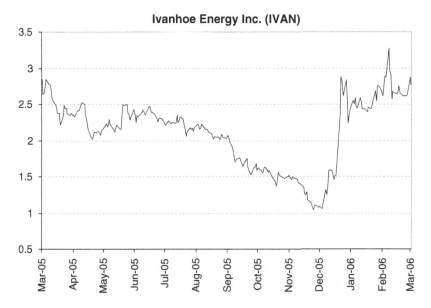

Ivanhoe Energy Inc. (IVAN)

13. *Is your stock a good candidate for the January effect?* If so, the odds favor the trade. There are many examples of stocks that rise in January. Take a quick look at Oscient Pharmaceuticals (OSCI). Here's a stock that made a steady rise to its January highs. There are many others that one could cite.

14. *Are you buying when most of the news on the stock is negative?* The correct time to buy a stock is when no one wants it. The stock's story is known, the bloom is off the rose, and the cream of the move has already been skimmed by savvy investors. In the example of Ivanhoe Energy, the stock registered a low of just 99 cents on December 22, 2005, with a close of $1.04 a share. Less than a month later, on January 19, 2006, IVAN traded as high as $3.42, a 345 percent gain! Looking back, here are just four comments made by IVAN bulletin board posters on Yahoo Finance: First, the positive statements: "You will never get another chance." "Time to buy with both hands." But the stock's detractors would have none of it: "All U dummies thinking you are buying the bottom, think again"—this when the stock was trading at $1.35 a share. Finally, an investor who noticed the pickup in volume had this to say: "Volume today means either someone in the know just bought

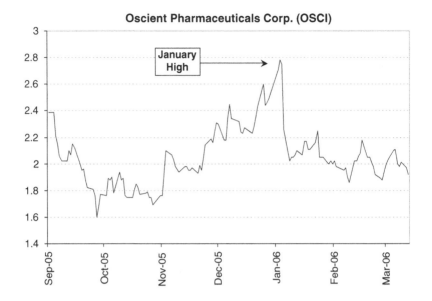

from those who are sick of the stock's performance—Or someone is getting clear the hell away from a drop which is coming soon." The rest is history.

Differences of opinion make the market. It seems that this statement is a fitting way to end our discussion of buying small stock for big profits. You can never be sure that you are right. But you can never be right unless you take on the risk. Clearly, many are called. But how many are chosen? You need to provide your own answer.

THE LOOK AHEAD

As someone who has been investing and speculating in stocks, options, and futures for almost 40 years, I can tell you that spectacular gains can come from investing in low-priced stocks. For the uninitiated, of course, these investments can be downright dangerous. Nevertheless, on balance, I have to stress that inexpensive stocks can be extremely gratifying. In recent years, the small caps have run both hot and cold. At times, the markets in these stocks get really hot; at other times, you have to be careful. Regardless of where we are in the cycle when you begin investing in these stocks, you must remember one thing: Over the long haul, this has been the best-performing segment of the market, *rising an encouraging 12.8 percent on an annualized basis since 1925.* That's a total of more than 80 years!

At the same time, the risk, which is often perceived to be quite high in these issues, has declined. That's because of the growth in markets especially suited to these smaller companies and because of technological breakthroughs. You no longer have to be a General Motors or Penn Central Railroad to attract investor capital. Today, a young entrepreneur with an idea can gain the attention of Wall Street, find financing for the idea, and put it to the test. Success or failure will depend on the entrepreneur's vision and inner drive. Fortunately, investors of even modest means can join in the growth of these small companies and likewise share in the excitement of seeing their investment grow.

Risk can never be eliminated from the investment arena, nor would you want it to be. Where there is uncertainty, there is risk. And what is more uncertain than a company with a new idea trying to get off the ground? I recently read an article about the growth in new modular homes. Stylishly designed, these new homes are about as different as they could possibly be from their nearest cousin, the classic double-wide mobile home. Benefiting from economies of scale and new materials coming on the market, these homes give the traditional stick-built structures a very competitive run for the money. Will there be new start-up companies entering this field? You bet. This is the type of idea that can lead to a great stock investment.

In the past 10 years alone, we have seen enhanced electronically available information, increased liquidity, and a greater flow of capital. These and other improvements could very well result in a sustained bull market for emerging new companies.

What are some of the factors that could fuel this coming bull market? Here are a few suggestions:

- Continued emphasis on the lowering of capital gains taxes. As we have increasingly become an investors' society, capital gain taxes are no longer just for the rich.
- New laws to encourage long-term savings such as Keogh accounts, IRAs, and Roth IRAs. As more investment funds become available and more money flows into capital markets, the market averages should rise.
- A simplified tax code. This should help both investors and small companies free up money to invest.
- The growth of electronic stock exchanges with investment activities for a global audience and open for business 24 hours a day.
- The growth of hedge funds and venture capital firms.
- The growth of the Internet, which has leveled the playing field in the investment world.

The material covered in these pages should just be a start for the new investor. Some 40 years ago, I went into a brokerage house in New York

City and asked to speak with a broker. Uranium stocks were all the rage back then, and I remember walking out as the proud owner of 100 shares of this hot, new uranium stock that I had read about. How little did I know how much there was to learn. Ever since, I've been hooked on the investment world. If I've done my job here, there will be readers who will grow to share my enthusiasm for these exciting markets.

The making of a successful investor is a process, not an event. Hopefully, the material presented here will enable the reader to speed up that process and master the inevitable learning curve that every new investor must make. Here's to excellent rewards in your stock selections in the years ahead! Happy investing!

About the Author

George Angell is the author of eight books on trading, including *Winning in the Futures Market* and *Sure-Thing Options Trading*. In addition, Angell lectures on the futures and options markets and creates software, audiotapes, and videotapes on trading strategy. He has appeared on CNBC and CBS television, as well as numerous radio shows. He spent 10 years as a floor trader in Chicago and is a graduate of New York University.

Index

Covad Communications Group, 46, 47, 169
  price chart for, 170
  seasonal trend with, 106, 108
Cover, for prospectus, 130
CPST. *See* Capstone Turbine
Cray Research, xii
Cup and handle chart pattern, 31
Current assets, 153
Current liabilities, 153
Current replacement costs, 153
Current value, determining, 145
CUR.TO. *See* DiagnoCure
Cyclical market, Kulicke and Soffa Industries: example of, 66–67

Danka Business Systems (DANKY), 85, 86
Day-of-the-week strategies, 115, 116
Debt, 155–156
Dell, 142
Democratic Republic of Congo, 5
Depreciation allowance, 153–154
Depressed stocks, buying, 1, 4, 135, 168–169, 172–173
Descending triangle chart pattern, 32
Desert Sun Mining (DEZ), first leg for, 175, 176
Deteriorating markets, characteristics of, 25
DiagnoCure, 6, 7
Diamonds, 29
Dickens, Charles, 125
Dilution, prospectus and, 130
Dips, buying on, 42
Discipline, 65
Disclosure, 126, 129
Disney, 9, 15, 46, 56, 74, 160
Distribution phase, 36
Diversification, 57
Dividend policy, in prospectus, 130
Dollar cost averaging, 147
Double tops and bottoms, 32
Dow Chemical, options example, 157
Downtrends, 34

DRC. *See* Democratic Republic of Congo
DRDGold(DROOY): first and second legs of, 175, 176
Dull volume, 87
DVW. *See* Covad Communications Group

Earnings, revenues and, 148–149
Earnings before interest, taxes, depreciation, and amortization, 150
Earnings reports, 52, 56
Ebbers, Bernard, 56
EBITDA. *See* Earnings before interest, taxes, depreciation, and amortization
Engex (EGX), 178
Enron, 33, 56, 83
Equilibrium price, 35, 83
Equinox Minerals (EQN.TO), xiii
Escalon Medical Corp. (ESMC), 70, 72
Euro Tech Holdings, 70, 71
Exhaustion gaps, 32, 36
Explosive growth, 68
Extreme Networks, Inc. (EXTR), 85

False breakouts, 25, 28
Fibonacci, 88
Fibonacci numbers, 20
Fibonacci 0.618 retracement, 88, 95
  aggressive buying and, 60, 61
  countermoves and, 88, 89, 90, 91
52-week highs and lows, 42
Filters, trading, 115–119
Final allocation, 132
Financial statements, 150
First leg, 192
  identifying, 173–178
  of the trend, 35
First Quantum Minerals, ix, xiv, 2–3, 3, 5, 142
5-day average, of stock's range, 120
5-day oscillator, 114, 115, 116, 193
  3-day difference in, 112
  formula for, 111

Printed in the United States
By Bookmasters